PRAYER

PRAYER

A PRIMER

Henry F. French

Augsburg Books
Minneapolis

PRAYER
A Primer

Cover art: pebbles, © Giacomo Nodari/iStockphoto.
Cover design: Christy Barker
Interior design: Michelle L. N. Cook

Library of Congress Cataloging-in-Publication Data
French, Henry F.
  Prayer : a primer / Henry F. French.
    p. cm.
  Includes bibliographical references (p.   ).
  ISBN 978-0-8066-5766-0 (alk. paper)
  1. Prayer—Christianity. I. Title.
  BV215.F763 2009
  248.4—dc22   2008055045

Manufactured in the U.S.A.

I dedicate this book

to my *anam cara*

"soul friend"

love and music of my life

Bobbi

CONTENTS

ACKNOWLEDGMENTS

Every book such as this emerges out of the totality of the author's experiences and relationships. To properly acknowledge the people who have influenced this book, I would have to acknowledge every person I have ever interacted with. What I have experienced and who I have experienced define me. It being impossible to name them all, let me acknowledge a few categories of people and a few individuals whose influence has been most profound.

- The retreat masters who have taught me and encouraged me.
- The writers whose works have taught and inspired me.
- The parishioners for whom I have prayed and who have prayed for me in the "school of prayer" known as the church.
- The meditation groups I have been a part of.
- Those to whom I have given spiritual direction who have, in turn, done the same for me.
- My seminary students in Japan and America who have asked me probing and relevant questions.

And then the individuals:

- My wife Bobbi, who read the manuscript, commented, and kept me honest as only she can do.
- My children, Jason, Kirstin, Andy, and Michael, who always asked "How's it going?"
- Gloria Bengtson at Augsburg Fortress Publishers, editor and friend who had the vision for the book and encouraged its writing.
- Susan Johnson at Augsburg Fortress Publishers who brought the book from final editing to the printer.
- My good friend Ron Klug, who brought his editorial skills to bear on the manuscript to great effect.
- Bill Smith, teacher and spiritual guide.

Thanks to all.

INTRODUCTION

For God alone my soul waits in silence;
from him comes my salvation.
—Psalm 62:1

Although just now putting pen to paper (actually, fingers to keyboard), I have been writing this little book for decades. Even as a child, God fascinated me, and the idea of communicating with God, of knowing God and following God intrigued me. I don't think I am unusual. Very young children seem to be more open and accepting than most adults when it comes to wonder, mystery, magic, and miracle. Children seem to sense sacredness. They seem to be aware of the divine dimensions of reality; they seem to perceive things that most modern adults have long forgotten or dismissed as childish fantasy.

Children seem relatively filter free when it comes to perceiving the supernatural within the natural. They have not yet learned from a largely rationalistic and materialistic culture to filter out and dismiss intimations of the Divine. They have not yet had their vision distorted by skepticism and cynicism, clouded by distrust and doubt, dimmed by fear and feelings of estrangement from the universe. Perhaps that is why Jesus told his followers: "Truly I tell you, unless you change and become like children, you will never enter the kingdom of heaven" (Matthew 18:3). The trick is not for adults to become childish, but to become childlike. The many ways of prayer can help with that for they open us once again to the childlike sense of wonder and mystery that most of us lost or were in the process of losing by the time we entered first grade.

As children grow from toddlerhood to adulthood, they travel away from "home," away from a feeling of oneness, of deep connection with both the natural and the supernatural, and toward an increasing sense of separation, of alienation and, therefore, of threat. The very young experience little fear; for most adults, fear (often disguised) is the motivating force for almost everything we do. Prayer can assuage fear and turn us back toward the "home" we knew as children when all was right with the world and life was lived in the mutuality of love. As you will discover as you work your way through this little book, prayer has to do with love, and "there is no fear in love" (1 John 4:18a).

SPIRITUALITY AS A JOURNEY

Perhaps the most common metaphor for the spiritual life is that of a journey. In books, magazines, sermons, and conversations between Christians, it is not uncommon to hear comments and questions about the "journey of faith." Everyone, it seems, either is or ought to be on a faith journey. Indeed, it is difficult to find a book on spirituality that doesn't use this metaphor.

The reason is obvious—the metaphor of a journey resonates with our experience. It points to a basic existential truth: *we feel somehow lost*, alienated from ourselves, each other, the world, God. We are like strangers in a strange land searching for that place we can finally call home. As the writer to the Hebrews put it, we are "strangers and foreigners on the earth . . . seeking a homeland" (11:13).

Although the language is a bit outdated, an old nineteenth-century hymn says it well:

I'm a pilgrim, and I'm a stranger,
I can tarry, I can tarry but a night;
Do not detain me, for I am going
To where the fountains are ever flowing.

There the glory is ever shining;
Oh, my longing heart, my longing heart is there;
Here in this country so dark and dreary,
I long have wandered forlorn and weary.

There's the city to which I journey;
My Redeemer, my Redeemer is its Light;
There is no sorrow nor any sighing,
Nor any tears there, nor any dying. [1]

The hymn reflects a strong biblical motif—the human yearning for God and for a place where God "will wipe every tear from [our] eyes. Death will be no more; mourning and crying and pain will be no more, for the first things have passed away" (Revelation 21:4). Or as the Hebrew poet put it: "As a deer longs for flowing streams, so my soul longs for you, O God. My soul thirsts for God, for the living God. When shall I come and behold the face of God?" (Psalm 42:1-2). Most of us know something about such longing—it is behind our own spiritual journeys. It is in a profound sense the longing to be loved and to love.

The image of the journey is powerful precisely because it speaks to our deepest experience and our deepest fears—the experience of being lost a long way from Eden and the fear that, as sojourners in a dark land of pain, grief, and death, we may never find the way back. Even in an affluent culture like ours with its seemingly endless supply of material, emotional, psychological, and sensual pleasures, the journey toward the sacred beckons millions of people who have the inescapable sense that all those pleasures are transient, insubstantial, and finally unsatisfactory. We look for more, and the "more" seems to be out there, ahead of us, in the distance, at journey's end. From birth to death, from baptism to resurrection, life is a journey towards God. It is true, and so the journey motif works. But it is not the only metaphor that speaks to our deep spiritual experience.

SPIRITUALITY AS SEEING

Those who set out on a journey of faith (and this book is largely about doing just that on the path of prayer) often discover along the way that—in a profound sense—*there is nowhere to go*. God is not out there at journey's end. As Paul told the Athenians, "Indeed he is not far from each one of us. For 'In him we live and move and have our being'" (Acts 17:27b-28). God is ubiquitous, everywhere present. Again, we find a strong biblical motif:

> Where can I go from your spirit?
> Or where can I flee from your presence?
> If I ascend to heaven, you are there;
> > if I make my bed in Sheol, you are there.
> If I take the wings of the morning
> > and settle at the farthest limits of the sea,
> even there your hand shall lead me,
> > and your right hand shall hold me fast. (Psalm 139:7-10)

So, it is not so much a question of *finding* God as it is a question of becoming *aware* of God's presence to us, with us, and within us. Always. Everywhere. Profoundly, the journey is a pilgrimage in which you learn to *see* that "your body is a temple of the Holy Spirit within you, which you have from God, and that you are not your own" (1 Corinthians 6:19). It is a pilgrimage in which you come to truly *see* God in the other (Matthew 25:40); a pilgrimage in which the whole world becomes transparent to the ubiquity of God (Romans 1:19-20).

Jesus said:

The eye is the lamp of the body. So, if your eye is healthy, your whole body will be full of light; but if your eye is unhealthy, your whole body will be full of darkness. If then the light in you is darkness, how great is the darkness! (Matthew 6:22-23)

For most of us it must be said that our eyes are not healthy. We do not *see* the sacred within the secular, the divine within the ordinary, the holy within the commonplace, God "who fills all in all" (Ephesians 1:23). Spirituality, then, is profoundly about seeing, about learning to see, about recovering healthy eyes and a body full of light. That too, is what this book is about—prayer as a path of seeing, a path of awareness. It is no accident that much of Jesus' ministry had to do with restoring the sight of the blind (Luke 4:18). Take that literally if you will, but don't miss the clear metaphorical meaning either.

SPIRITUALITY—A TWOFOLD JOURNEY

So, we are on two simultaneous journeys. On the one hand, we are indeed living "east of Eden," journeying toward wherever life will take us beyond our inevitable death. It is a journey through ambiguity, through sorrow and joy, through grief and celebration, through suffering and sensuality—but faith trusts that it is, paradoxically, a journey both with and to God.

On the other hand, we are on a journey toward awareness, toward wisdom, toward the consciousness of God, toward *seeing* and understanding that the kingdom of God is not a geographical place to go, that the kingdom is not at journey's end. In Jesus' words: "For, in fact, the kingdom of God is among [and within] you" (Luke 17:20b).[2] The kingdom can (and should) be lived in—in the here and now, in the present moment.

This book is about prayer as the path upon which we take this twofold journey. It is an invitation to begin moving and begin seeing.

WHAT GOD WANTS FOR YOU AND FROM YOU

As you work your way through this little book—and I emphasize the word "work," for the only way to learn prayer is by praying—you will discover that it is focused not so much on what we want from God but on what God wants for and from us. In the Sermon on the Mount, Jesus talks about our many worries about what we will eat and what we will drink and what we will wear—metaphors for the many anxieties, desires, cares and distractions that constantly consume us. He suggests that "life is more than food and the body more than clothing." Then he concludes by saying that God knows what we need and that rather than focus on that we should "strive first for the kingdom of God and his righteousness, and all these things will be given to you as well" (Matthew 6:25-33).

That takes trust. Prayer builds trust because prayer builds the relationship between us and God. And that is one of the things God wants both for us and from us. Prayer also is a way of striving for the kingdom of God and God's righteousness—and that also is what God wants for us and from us.

At the heart of this book lies an Old Testament text that is perhaps the best one-line description of the Christian life of faith that you can find anywhere:

> He [God] has told you, O mortal, what is good;
>   and what does the LORD require of you
> but to do justice, and to love kindness,
>   and to walk humbly with your God? (Micah 6:8)

God wants you to experience justice. God wants you to be treated fairly, to have sufficient amounts of the material necessities of life, to be free of oppression and exploitation, to live safe from the threat and harm inflicted by those who place their own hunger and thirst for power, position, possessions, and privilege over the dignity and right to a full life of others. That's what God wants for you and that's what God wants from you—justice. "Blessed are those who hunger and thirst for righteousness . . ." (Matthew 5:6a). As you will discover in this little book, prayer and justice go hand in hand.

But God does not only want you to be treated justly; God also wants you to be treated kindly. God wants you to experience kindness, love, compassion, mercy, forgiveness, generosity, gentleness—and that is what God wants from you in your relationships with others. As you will also discover in this little book, prayer and kindness go hand in hand.

And finally, God wants a relationship with you—for your sake and for God's sake. At its most profound level, the Bible can be seen as the story of God's longing for a mutually conscious relationship with humankind grounded in the mutuality of love. As I hope you will discover in this little book, prayer is the way of love, and thus the way to an ever growing, ever deepening relationship with God.

Learning prayer as a path to justice, a path to loving kindness, and a path to relationship with God requires at the outset no more than a commitment to pray. It is the place to begin—and that is where this book will begin—with chapter one, "Getting Started in Prayer."

THREE CONCLUDING INTRODUCTORY REMARKS

First, you have probably already noticed that in this short Introduction there are many references to biblical texts. This book is about *Christian* prayer, and the Christian life of faith is grounded in the Old and New Testaments. Prayer is at the heart of the life of faith, and so it is important that those who want to pray as Christians be grounded in the Old and New Testaments in general and in the Gospels in particular. Let me suggest that when you come across a biblical reference in this book, you take the time to look it up in the Bible and spend a few moments meditating on its meaning in its context. Let me also suggest that along with this book you read through the four Gospels, Matthew, Mark, Luke, and John. They tell us what we can know about this first century Jewish man whose consciousness of God and understanding of the will of God provide the foundational disclosure of what God wants for us and from us. The story of Jesus' life and death and resurrection are the soil from which a vibrant life of prayer grows. Read the Gospels. If you haven't been in the habit of doing so, you may be surprised as to what they have to say about the God to whom you pray.

Second, when I speak about "Jesus" in this book, I am talking about Jesus of Nazareth, the historical Jesus, the pre-resurrection Jesus. When I speak about Christ, I am speaking about the post-resurrection Jesus, the Christ of faith, the Jesus whose presence has been continually experienced in the community of faith after his death, right up to today, tomorrow, and beyond. When I speak about God, Christ, Holy Spirit, or just Spirit, I am speaking about one mystery, for as the ancient Israelites declared: "Hear O Israel: The LORD our God, the LORD is one" (Deuteronomy 6:4). This One we call God, disclosed in Jesus of Nazareth, present as living Christ and Holy Spirit, invites us through prayer into the mystery of divine love where we will see both God and ourselves as if for the first time.

Third, at the back of the book you will find questions for reflection, journaling suggestions, and suggestions for practice for each chapter. After finishing a chapter, I suggest that you work through them before moving on to the next chapter. They will help you think through what you have read and practice what you have learned. As my wife Bobbi told one of her young violin students who defended not practicing by saying that "Practice doesn't make perfect," "Well, practice might not make perfect, but practice does make progress!" So remember, the key to awakening to the mystery of God and yourself is practice, practice, practice. That's your part. Divine grace will do the rest.

HENRY F. FRENCH
Terra Sophia at Giese, Minnesota
July 22, 2008, Feast of Mary Magdalene, Apostle

one

GETTING STARTED
IN PRAYER

As a deer longs for flowing streams
so my soul longs for you, O God
—Psalm 43:1

It might seem strange to start a book about prayer with a chapter titled "Getting Started in Prayer." After all, haven't most Christians at least "started?" Is there any person of faith who has never prayed—no matter how haltingly? Is there any person of faith who has never gotten stuck, sick, or scared and not asked God for help? Is there anyone who in one way or another has never called out to God in times of joy and celebration or in times of distress and despair? Haven't most of us memorized the Lord's Prayer and maybe a table grace or two? Didn't most who grew up in a Christian family learn to pray "Now I lay me down to sleep; I pray the Lord my soul to keep" (or something similar) before going to sleep? The answer, of course, is yes. Most of us have indeed prayed in such ways, but that is not the same as really getting started in prayer.

If prayer is something done rarely and usually only when you need something you can't get or make happen for yourself, you haven't really gotten started in prayer. If prayer is largely a mechanical repetition of memorized or written prayers during a worship service, you haven't really gotten started in prayer. If you prayed as a child but now feel uncomfortable, if not childish, talking to God, you haven't gotten started in prayer. If you feel that prayer is a practice best left to religious professionals or the "pious" among us, you haven't gotten started in prayer—even if you try to (or are compelled to) pray from time to time.

THE JOURNEY OF A THOUSAND MILES

An ancient Chinese proverb states: "The journey of a thousand miles begins with the first step." It is an apt metaphor for getting started in prayer. The metaphor assumes that, as important as the first step is, it is the journey that matters, and it is the expectation of what will be experienced and known on the journey, as well as the vision of journey's end, that sustains the traveler.

Without the first step, there is no journey and no journey's end. Without the first step, there are no new experiences, no new sights, no new knowledge and understanding. Without the first step, we stay where we are.

But that's not where most of us want to be. To one degree or another, we long for God. We have a *built-in desire* to be close to the God in whose image we were all created. For some it is an unconscious desire; for others it is a desire of which they are only occasionally and perhaps dimly aware; for others it is a deep and always present longing. What is it for you? Where on the spectrum of desire for God do you experience yourself? I suspect that were you not to some extent aware of such a desire you would not be reading this book.

At the beginning of this chapter I quoted an ancient Hebrew poet who beautifully wrote, "As a deer longs for flowing streams, so my soul longs for you, O God." It is completely natural for deer to long for and seek out the fresh, clear and clean water of a flowing stream—it's not something they have to think about. It is just as natural for your soul to long for and seek out God.

When being hunted by a predator, startled by a hunter, or caught in the glare of approaching headlights, a deer can be distracted from and temporarily forget about its longing for flowing streams, but the longing is still there—beneath the threshold of immediate consciousness, but there, ready to surface when the distractions are gone, ready to turn the deer again towards life-giving water. And so it is with us and our longing for God.

The distractions and worries of modern life are too many to mention. The many duties, demands, and obligations that we assume or that are forced on us seem to control our lives and blur our focus. The enticements of pleasure, power, position, and privilege lay claim to our attention. The lure of getting and keeping wealth and possessions limits our vision. The real and imagined fears, threats, and dangers of modern life constrict our thoughts, attitudes, and behaviors. Obsessive compulsive and addictive behaviors anesthetize us to the uncertainty, the pain, the fear, the overload of life in these times, and in doing so, numb our awareness of things outside ourselves.

Like a deer in danger, we too can be distracted from and forget our longing for God. But the longing is still there—beneath the level of immediate consciousness perhaps, or only dimly, vaguely felt, but there, ready to turn us toward God. Prayer, as you will discover, is a way of dealing with these distractions and worries; it gives us a new perspective on them.

Over time, the path of prayer will change the way you see things, will change the way you experience things, will change the way you experience yourself and God. The path of prayer will teach you what the Psalmist meant when he or she wrote: "For with you [God] is the fountain of life; in your light we see light" (Psalm 36:9). This is all the reason anyone should need for setting out on the "journey of a thousand miles," for getting started in prayer.

The journey may actually begin with the first step, but all journeys are set in motion by a sense that it is *time to go*, time to take that first step. In the path of prayer, the sense that it is time to go emerges out of the simple awareness of your soul's longing for God. It's always there, but you need to feel it and affirm it.

SETTING THE JOURNEY IN MOTION

Read the next four paragraphs and then close the book for as long as it takes you to complete the exercise.

Sit comfortably with your back straight, eyes closed, hands in your lap. Breathe through your nose and focus your attention on your nostrils. Don't try to control your breath; just feel it coming in and going out. If you get distracted and your attention wanders, just gently bring it back to your breath. Remember that breath is a gift of God, the gift of life itself (Genesis 2:7; Psalm 104:29-30).

The purpose of this little exercise is to use the breath as a point of focus to still the mind of its many distractions and to open you to the awareness of God (Psalms 46:10a). We will talk more about using the breath to get centered in prayer in chapters five and seven; for now simply let the awareness of your breathing calm your mind.

Once you feel collected and settled, begin to meditate on your longing for God. Be very honest with yourself. Prayer demands honesty. Can you feel your longing for God? If so, what does it feel like? How strong is it? What is its emotional tone? How would you describe it to another person? How important to you is it? If you cannot feel your longing for God, can you imagine such a longing? If so, meditate on what you imagine to be your longing for God.

When your meditation has run its course, offer a few words to God simply affirming your desire for God. It doesn't matter how strongly or weakly you presently feel your longing for God; what matters is simply that you acknowledge it (however you experience it) before God. God will take it from there.

THE FIRST STEP

With the awareness and acknowledgement of your longing for God, your journey on the path of prayer is set in motion. Nothing remains but to take the first step. Reading this (or any other) book on prayer is not the first step. This book is simply a travel guide for those who have taken the first step . . . and the second . . . and the third. . . .

The first step is simply to *commit yourself* to the path of prayer. It is not a commitment to read about prayer, or study prayer, or even think about prayer. It is a commitment to pray. To do it. And to do it until it is no longer what you do, it is who you are.

Some thirty-four years ago, while still a seminary student, I had a crisis of faith over the place of prayer in my life of faith (more on this in chapter seven). The crisis was resolved and prayer became important to me in ways it had never been before. My renewed interest in prayer drove me to libraries and bookstores, and I began to read both modern and classical texts on prayer. In one of those books (I don't remember which one) I read an anecdote about Thomas Merton, one of the deepest practitioners and teachers of Christian spirituality and prayer of the last century.

According to the story, when Merton came to faith as an adult he developed a passionate interest in prayer. He would come home from the library with a stack of books about prayer and the Christian spiritual life, work through them, return them, and come home with another stack. One day, as he reached for the top book on the latest stack, he heard God saying to him: "Thomas, don't you think it is time to stop reading about prayer and start praying?" I laughed, right out loud. It could have been me.

It is easy to get intellectually fascinated by something that is really not intellectual at all. It is also easy to let intellectual fascination become a means of avoidance, a way of avoiding the "work" of prayer. "If I read one more book, then I will better know how to do it and how to do it right!" The trouble is, there is always one more book. As has been well said: "Of making many books there is no end, and much study is a weariness of the flesh" (Ecclesiastes 12:12). I have known too many people over the years whose enthusiasm for prayer was diminished to nothing because instead of praying they did no more than read about praying.

You can read every book ever written about dancing, about its history, about its many forms, about the physiology and psychology of it, about its meaning in human culture—but if you've never been on the dance floor, you don't know what dancing is, haven't got a clue. The same is true of prayer. (I hope that this book does not become a means of avoidance, or a "weariness of the flesh" for you. It won't, I believe, if you use it only as a travel guide, a map to territory you are walking *on your own two feet*.)

And so the first step on the path of prayer is the commitment to actually pray and to learn the ways of prayer by praying. So, if you are ready, let's take it. If you're not ready, keep reading. If you later become ready, take a moment to follow this suggestion:

Put the book down for a moment, and take the first step on the path of prayer by praying, by telling God of your commitment to become a person of prayer.

EARLY OBSTACLES TO PRAYER

This might be a good place to confront head-on two obstacles to continuing on the path of prayer that are commonly experienced by people of faith who have taken or are considering taking the first step. If you are experiencing either or both of these obstacles, there is no need to feel bad about it. It casts no shadow over your faith. I have experienced these obstacles myself, and have talked with countless others who have also experienced them, and I view them as a rather normal occurrence for people who take their faith seriously and are faced with the call and desire to grow in it.

Not knowing what to do or how to do it

I have taught classes on prayer for many years, led many contemplative prayer (meditation) groups, and done one-on-one spiritual direction with many good people who wanted to deepen their life of faith. More often than not, during the first class, group session, or conversation, most participants would express a feeling of intimidation or inadequacy, a sense that maybe they shouldn't be doing this, a fear of failure.

I know the feeling. Prayer has to do with God, and when dealing with God many have a sense that it's important to get it right, and, if you can't get it right, you ought not to try. Leave it to others (pastors, other professional Christians, the "pious") who know what they are doing. That feeling has kept many people who long for a deeper connection with God out of prayer classes, meditation groups, and spiritual direction—until, that is, their longing for God gets the better of them and with some "fear and trembling" they take the risk and "show up."

As Woody Allen shrewdly observed, "Eighty percent of success is showing up." That is particularly true when it comes to prayer. Showing up is risky, it leaves you vulnerable. Prayer requires vulnerability. Prayer is the heart of our relationship with God, and no relationship works without a willingness to be vulnerable. I am never concerned by feelings of vulnerability in people who are interested in prayer; when such people don't feel vulnerable, then I get concerned.

A few years ago, I invited a middle-aged man (we'll call him Harry) to sit over a cup of coffee and talk about prayer. I had known Harry for some time and had experienced him as both sincere and questioning, as someone whose faith was becoming more and more central to how he understood himself. He was increasingly active in the church and rarely missed a Sunday worship service. I had invited him to join a class on prayer. He had respectfully declined. But he did accept my invitation to coffee and conversation.

We sat down at the neighborhood deli and, after a exchanging a few pleasantries, I came right to the point. I asked why he had turned down my invitation to the class. His answer was also right to the point:

"Two reasons. First, I'm uncomfortable talking about my faith in front of others. I believe, but I've got a lot of questions and I don't like to talk publically about something until I've got it straight. I don't have it straight yet. Second, it's a class on prayer, and I don't know anything about that. I don't know *what* to do, and I wouldn't know *how* to do it if I did."

Harry's response had a refreshing honesty to it, and if not a willingness to be vulnerable, it showed a clear sense of vulnerability.

"Do you know how to talk?" I asked him.

I think my question took him by surprise. Instead of answering, he just looked quizzical.

"If you know how to talk," I said, "then you know how to pray. That's all prayer is—talking, talking to God (or being silent with God) the same way you talk to (or are silent with) your wife, kids, friends, co-workers. Of course, that doesn't mean you couldn't stand to improve your communication skills—that's what the class is all about—but if you can talk, you can pray, and if you know how to be silent and still be connected to another, you can pray."

The conversation went on for a while and then ended with: "I'll think about it." He was there on Tuesday night—still uncomfortable, feeling vulnerable, but he showed up.

Although prayer may take you deep into the mystery of God, there is nothing magical about it—except, that is, the "magic" of a relationship grounded in mutual love and trust. There are no secret or arcane things to learn, no esoteric rites or practices, no theological or philosophical mountains to climb. Just talk to God (in everyday language) when you need to talk—and be silent in God's presence when silence says it all.

The fear of taking God more seriously

Most people who call themselves Christian take God with some seriousness. They worship, receive the sacrament of bread and wine, participate in church programs, serve on committees, provide their children (if they have any) with Christian education. They wonder, if not worry, about their values and behavior in the light of what they know about God's will. They do all this because God matters to them, and their eternal destiny, which they believe rests in God's hands, also matters to them. And yet, it is not uncommon for people who take God with some seriousness to wonder, if not worry, about what would happen to them if they took God *more* seriously than they do now.

This seems a good time to raise the question: can God be taken *too* seriously? I don't think so. It could, of course, be argued that all the ways that life is diminished or damaged or destroyed everyday all around the world, in one or another of the names of God, is a good example of taking God too seriously. I would disagree. That is a case of taking power or politics or economic advantage or some ideology or theology too seriously, not God.

In such cases, "God"—and the violent defense of both God and the "will" of God—is little more than the mask behind which we hide our own baser instincts. Psychologically, prayer to the god who sanctions such violence is *prayer to oneself*. It is an attempt to justify to oneself and to others the mean-spiritedness, the brutishness, the greed, and lust for power, in any or all of their many forms, that make such a mess of God's good creation. Under the veneer of religion we take ourselves—not God—too seriously, claiming divine sanction to justify all manner of violence. God is love (1 John 4:8, 16), and love can never be taken too seriously. It can always be taken more seriously.

And yet, the fear of taking God more seriously is often given as a reason for not taking prayer seriously. To take prayer seriously is to leave the comfortable for what might not be so comfortable, and who wants to do that?

Many years ago, while I was living and working in Japan, I sat over sushi with a good friend. He was a professor at a theological seminary, a teacher of church history, a good preacher with a fine sense of worship. As I munched on a piece of squid that was a bit too chewy, I complimented him on the beautiful prayer he had spoken as the leader of the seminary's chapel service that morning. Here was a man with impressive academic credentials, who relished his role in liturgical worship, and was sought after as a guest preacher. As we continued to talk about things religious, I mentioned how important prayer was becoming to me—particularly contemplative or meditative prayer.

He looked at me over his cup of green tea and said, "That's not for me. Liturgical prayer on Sunday is all I want."

I asked him, "Why?"

"Because I like things just the way they are."

"Uh, you want to explain that a little more?" I asked.

"Sure," he said. "I just have this sense that if I get serious about prayer, I will find myself getting more serious about God, and I'm not sure I want to do that."

"Why not?"

"Why not? Because if I really take God more seriously, I'll probably have to go places I don't want to go and do things I don't want to do!"

It was an "aha" moment. He had given voice to feelings I have also had (and to some extent still do). It reminded me of what Father Daniel Berrigan, Jesuit priest and social activist, said back in the 1960s: "If you want to follow Jesus, you better learn to look good on wood." Which is precisely why so many of us don't follow Jesus and the world continues to be in the mess it is.

I respected my friend's honesty, and over the years I've heard many others express similar sentiments. After all, having taken a few steps on a thousand mile journey and then looking down the road, one cannot see too far, and it is easy to imagine that the journey will be arduous and indeed might take us where we don't really want to go.

Jesus went where he didn't want to go. On the night of his betrayal, the night before his death on the cross, he prayed in the Garden of Gethsemane: "Father, if you are willing, remove this cup (suffering and death) from me . . ." (Luke 22:42). That's a perfectly good prayer when walking with God takes you places you would rather not be. It is a very human prayer. Jesus was human. But his prayer did not end there. He went on: "Yet, not my will but yours be done."

To pray as Jesus did requires radical trust in the complete goodness and love of God. It takes trusting that, in the words of Julian of
Norwich, no matter where walking with God takes you, and no matter what you might be asked to do along the way, "All will be well, all
will be well, all manner of things will be well."[3] It takes trusting that
what God said to Israel expresses God's intention for us as well: "For
surely I know the plans I have for you, says the LORD, plans for your
welfare and not for harm, to give you a future with hope" (Jeremiah
29:11).

Such trust does not come easy for us—fearful, insecure, uncer-
tain, sinful people that we are. While giving lip service to faith in the
goodness and love of God, we would rather rely on our own ability
to control the threats and promises of life. And so we do not "walk
[very] humbly with our God" (Micah 6:8).

As we get started in prayer, that's okay. And the fear of what
might happen to us if we take God with more seriousness ought not
to be an obstacle to getting started. If you are just getting started in
prayer, or have been walking the path of prayer for a short time, *you
cannot trust completely* in the goodness and love of God, and so you
shouldn't feel bad because you don't. Trust emerges over time and
out of relationship. Just keep walking the path of prayer, one foot in
front of the other, one step at a time, and trust will come. The only
way to get trust in another is through your own experience of the
other—and that goes for trust in God as well.

An unknown poet once wrote:

The will of God will never take you,
Where the grace of God cannot keep you.
Where the arms of God cannot support you,
Where the riches of God cannot supply your needs,
Where the power of God cannot endow you.
The will of God will never take you,
Where the spirit of God cannot work through you,
Where the wisdom of God cannot teach you. . . .

The will of God will never take you,
Where the love of God cannot enfold you . . .
Where the peace of God cannot calm your fears. . . .

It is true. But the only way to experience the truth of it and come to trust it is not by reading words on a page, but by your own experience walking with God—and that means walking the path of prayer.

LORD, TEACH US TO PRAY

According to Luke 11:1, once when Jesus had been praying, his followers came to him and said: "Lord, teach us to pray." He did—and he continues to teach his followers to pray. There is no point in taking the journey laid out in this book if you don't begin the journey with the rudimentary faith that you are not journeying alone. God is with and within you, leading, teaching, loving.

There is a great paradox in the New Testament. On the one hand, Paul writes that we are all "being transformed" into the image of Christ "from one degree of glory to another; for this comes from the Lord, the Spirit" (2 Corinthians 3:18). Notice that the verb is passive—we are *being* transformed, not transforming ourselves. The life of faith is not a pick-yourself-up-by-the-bootstraps affair. In the mystery of God's great love, we are being transformed by the Spirit of Christ into the image of Christ, transformed into fully human beings. It's grace, God's work.

On the other hand, however, Paul tells us that *we* must "work out [our] own salvation with fear and trembling; for it is God who is at work in [us], enabling [us] both to will and to work for his good pleasure" (Philippians 3:12b-13). There are things for us to do in the life of faith; God enables us to do what needs doing, but the doing is ours. We *can* pray; God is at work in us, enabling us to pray, enabling us to do justice, to love kindness, and to walk humbly with our God. The actual praying is ours to do. The justice, the kindness, the walk with God, are ours to do.

Before moving to the next chapter, move to the back of the book and ponder the questions. Spend some time journaling, and begin to practice, trusting that God is indeed at work in you, enabling you "both to will and to work for his good pleasure" which, in the way of things, is also our good pleasure.

BEGINNER'S MIND

Do not be conformed to this world,
but be transformed by the renewing of your minds,
so that you may discern what is the will of God—
what is good and acceptable and perfect.
—Romans 12:2

This chapter is about a certain way of being in the world that lends itself to a life of prayer. It is about a state of mind that is critically important for people who wish to grow spiritually, and growing spiritually is what prayer is all about.

If you are just starting to become a person of prayer, then you are a beginner. Beginners are by nature curious people. They know they have a lot to learn and are eager to do just that. But, no matter how curious and eager they are, they might well have to let go of a lot of what they already "know" in order to learn what they don't know.

In order to succeed in learning and following the way of prayer, you need to have what is known as "beginner's mind." A beginner's mind is an open mind, fresh and enthusiastic, with a deep sense of possibilities unfolding. A beginner's mind is not burdened with old habitual ways of thinking and acting, and so is open to new ways of thinking and acting.

A beginner's mind is in many ways a childlike mind. Children are always learning, and they don't let what they learn today stand in the way of learning something new—and possibly contradictory—tomorrow. Here we have another reason why Jesus insisted that unless we change and become like children, we will not enter the kingdom of heaven (Matthew 18:3). Young children have not yet developed into people who want to be known as "someone who knows;" they simply want to learn, to experience, to grow.

Young children do not have much if any baggage to get in the way of an open, curious, inquisitive, and guileless encounter with the world around them. They don't bring filters or interpretive lenses to their experience. They take what is as it is and let it teach them what it will. Such childlikeness in the face of all that is unknown is an essential quality for those who want to walk a spiritual path.

NOT ALL BEGINNERS HAVE BEGINNER'S MIND

It seems like it should not be at all difficult for those who are beginning something new to have a beginner's mind. But it is. I can remember being approached by a woman who wanted to learn about prayer. I told her that there were many kinds of prayer and as I listed them for her I mentioned contemplative prayer. She had never heard about it. I told her it was also called the prayer of silence in that it involved being still and silent before God. She said, "Is that like meditation?"

I answered, "Yes, many people use the words meditation and contemplation interchangeably."

She quickly responded, "Then don't tell me anything about it. I've heard that meditation empties the mind and when the mind is empty the devil can get in."

Well, meditation doesn't "empty" the mind, but she was in no mind to understand. She was a beginner, but she did not have beginner's mind. She had a mind burdened with preconceptions, a mind closed by opinions, beliefs, and biases that had been formed without the benefit of her own experience.

If you come to prayer with written-in-concrete opinions about what prayer is and is not, you will most likely not learn to pray. If you come to prayer holding expectations about what should or should not happen, you will most likely be disappointed. If you come to prayer with preconceived limits on what you are willing and not willing to experience, your prayer will likely remain shallow and one-dimensional. If you come to prayer with "beginner's mind," a spiritual path will open before you, a path into the mystery and presence of God.

BEGINNER'S MIND IS A STATE OF MIND

You know immediately when someone has beginner's mind—they are always asking questions of themselves and others. They can't help it. They are curious people. Their questions are not defensive, not designed to protect preconceived notions of what is and isn't true, of what's right and what's not. Their questions are not manipulative, not designed to mask their fears and uncertainties. People with beginner's mind ask questions of themselves and others simply because they don't know the answers and refuse to pretend that they do. Indeed, for people with beginner's mind, the questions are always more interesting than the answers because they know that for finite (and thus limited) people, all answers are tentative, subject to being refined or rejected on the basis of new experiences, new questions, and new insights.

German poet Rainer Marie Rilke's advice to a young poet is good advice for a person setting out on the path of prayer: "Be patient toward all that is unsolved in your heart and try to love the questions themselves. . . . Live the questions now. Perhaps you will then gradually, without noticing it, live along some distant day into the answer."[4]

Beginner's mind is a state of mind that is open, curious, not intimidated by seeming contradictions and paradoxes, eager to explore possibilities, at home with mystery. Beginner's mind is a state of mind that acknowledges vulnerability and is willing to take risks in order to "live the questions." It is an essential state of mind for a person of prayer because prayer is an encounter with the living God who cannot be contained in static "truths," concepts, or images. Prayer is an encounter with the living God who cannot be put into a conceptual box, cannot be domesticated, cannot be persuaded to act out our wishful thinking. To encounter this God is to be open to radical surprise. People with beginner's mind are always being surprised. People who think they already "know" are rarely, if ever, surprised.

If beginner's mind is a state of mind, a way of being in the world, a way of approaching life, then it would seem that either you have it or you don't. That's true. But if you don't have it, can you get it? Yes.

DEVELOPING BEGINNER'S MIND

If you want to have beginner's mind, you have to give up any hope or desire of becoming an "expert." As Shunryo Suzuki, a master in the tradition of Zen Buddhism, wrote in the prologue to his book, *Zen Mind, Beginner's Mind*: "In the beginner's mind there are many possibilities, but in the expert's there are few."[5]

A simple story will illustrate what I mean. A seminary professor makes an appointment with a spiritual director. He shows up on time, introduces himself, takes a chair, and says that he has heard that the spiritual director is wise in the ways of prayer and he would like to learn from her.

Before she can speak, however, our professor goes on to expound on all the things that he already "knows" about prayer. He moves on to discuss his pet theological notions, and then talks about his "wisdom" with respect to biblical "truth." He talks and talks and talks while the spiritual director simply smiles and listens. While the professor prattles on, she rises and walks over to a side table where a pot of coffee rests on a warmer. The professor keeps talking. She hands him an empty cup. He keeps talking. She takes her seat, leans toward him, he holds his cup out, and she begins pouring coffee into it. He keeps talking. The cup fills. She keeps pouring. He keeps talking. The coffee overflows and spills to the floor. Finally the professor stops talking. He jerks his cup away and cries out, "What in the world are you doing?"

"Call it a parable," she answers with a small smile. You are exactly like this cup—so full of yourself that there is no room to add anything else. You're wasting my time and yours."

She rises and opens the door to her office. "Feel free to come back if you ever figure out how to empty yourself a bit."

You should not want to become an expert in prayer. You should simply pray and see what happens; pray and be open to learning new things about God, the world, and yourself, things that may challenge what you think you know now. To develop beginner's mind, do not be afraid to change your mind. Serious prayer will call into question much of what you presently take for granted. It will change your relationship with God, your relationship with yourself, your relationships with family, friends, colleagues, and complete strangers. It will change your relationship to the natural world—in short, serious prayer will change your relationship to everything.

Do you want that to happen? It is an important question, and your ability to develop beginner's mind and to truly step out on the way of prayer hinges on the answer. If you are not willing to upset the applecart of cherished beliefs, long-held opinions, firm convictions, and the mix of prejudice and bias that color your view of just about everything, then you will never experience beginner's mind, and the power of prayer will most likely remain a mystery to you.

Perhaps you are beginning to sense that prayer is far more than simply asking God for things we can't get or make happen for ourselves or others. Prayer has to do with living in a relationship with God in which we are transformed more and more into Christ-likeness (2 Corinthians 3:17-18). Prayer has to do with learning to follow Jesus in the way of God that Jesus followed. Such learning will probably require a bit of unlearning.

Unlearning

To develop beginner's mind, start looking at things as if you hadn't seen them before; start reading things as if you hadn't read them before; start listening as if you hadn't heard before; start praying as if you hadn't prayed before. Look at the world, look at God, look at religion, look at the life of faith afresh, as if for the first time.

Marcus Borg, a Jesus scholar, wrote a book several years ago called *Meeting Jesus Again for the First Time*. It is a clever title and a remarkable book. It challenges us to "unlearn" much of what we think we know about Jesus in order to "meet" him again as if for the first time.

Borg followed his book on Jesus with one called *The God We Never Knew,* and then with one called *Reading the Bible Again for the First Time*—two more catchy titles and remarkable books that encourage us to unlearn, to rethink, to re-imagine our beliefs and convictions about God, Jesus, the Spirit, religious truth, and the life of faith.

Unlearning is driven by the premise that preconceived ideas can all too easily blind us from new or deeper understanding and prevent us from having new or deeper experiences. A good way to begin unlearning is to ask the simple question "What is . . ." of things we already think we know. What is faith? Write out a quick answer to the question that expresses your beliefs, convictions, and certainties about faith. Under your answer, in large letters, write: "Maybe so. Maybe not so." There are many basic questions whose answers we might need to unlearn in order to go deeper:

- What is prayer? Maybe so. Maybe not so.
- What is love? Maybe so. Maybe not so.
- What is forgiveness, what is salvation? Maybe so. Maybe not so.
- What is God's kingdom, what is justice? Maybe so. Maybe not so.
- What is the church? Maybe so. Maybe not so.
- What is worship? Maybe so. Maybe not so.
- Who is God? Maybe so. Maybe not so.
- Who is Jesus, who is the Spirit? Maybe so. Maybe not so.

This is not to be skeptical; it is to be quizzical, it is to love and live the questions into deeper answers that are themselves, in turn, questioned. Maybe so. Maybe not so.

TURNING TO THE BIBLE

Having raised the questions and jotted down what you think the answers are, you turn to the Bible and begin to read and take notes. Look for new insights, new ideas, new understandings, things you have never noticed before or have resisted noticing. Much in the Bible flies in the face of conventional wisdom. We are by and large conventional people and by and large resist having our conventional views challenged and changed. Hence the need for unlearning; hence the need for beginner's mind.

Start reading with the four Gospels. Take one of your "What is?" questions and read straight through Matthew, Mark, Luke, and John, writing down whatever answers to the question you find in the text. Read meditatively. Ponder individual words, sentences, paragraphs. Pay particular attention to things you've never noticed before. Check in with your reactions to what you find:

- Any excitement?
- Any resistance?
- Anything seem threatening?
- Anything seem challenging?
- Anything seem foolish or impractical or impossible?
- Any changes to your beliefs, attitudes, thinking, or action suggested?

If you answer yes to any of these questions, then don't forget to wonder why.

When you have finished reading through the gospels, read through your notes, summarize your conclusions, and then in large letters write: "Maybe so. Maybe not so." Then start to read the rest of the New Testament through the lens of your "What is?" question.

Continue taking notes. Read through your notes. Maybe so. Maybe not so.

It is an eye-opening, faith-changing experience to read through the Bible through the lens of one simple "What is?" question. You will most likely find much that you don't understand, but don't let that keep you from finding what you can understand. And when you have understood something, remember not to write it in stone. Possibly so, but possibly not so. Always be open to new learning that may challenge and change old learning. The next time you read through the New Testament, come at it as if for the first time and see what you find.

Once you have been through the New Testament asking one "What is?" question, choose another question and start over. And then another question and start over. And then another. And at some point you may want to go back to a question you have already asked and ask it again as you read through the New Testament again.

It may seem like a lot of work. It is. But it is work well worth doing. The Bible is the soil out of which a life of prayer grows. The deeper you dive into the Bible, the more likely it is that you will have in you the mind "that was in Christ Jesus" (Philippians 2:5). Keep bringing beginner's mind back to the Bible. Discover for yourself what it has to say, begin to discover for yourself what happens when you translate what it says into the way you live, into the way you do your relationships, into the way you make the decisions that get you from morning to night, into the way you pray.

BEGINNER'S MIND UNTIL YOU DIE

We are finite creatures, which means that we are limited creatures. No matter how much we learn, our knowledge will always be imperfect and incomplete. We can never fully comprehend or know Truth with a capital T. All our truths are small t truths, which means that all our truths are tentative, subject to new learning, new insight, new experience.

This is a very freeing idea. Too many people are virtual slaves to entrenched opinions, firmly held convictions, outdated ideas, and narrow points of view that they express as Truth with a capital T, beliefs that they must defend at all costs. Think of all the human misery that has been caused because one person's capital T truth is different from someone else's. Perhaps if we all had beginner's mind, if we were all able to follow the expression of our truth with "Maybe so. Maybe not so," then we could learn from each other rather than harm each other.

As you practice prayer and work through the Bible, your understanding will advance, but be careful to avoid the hubris of thinking that you are becoming an expert in prayer—it is the last thing you should want to be. No matter how "advanced" you are in prayer (or anything else) keep the childlike openness, the freshness, the inquisitiveness, the delight in learning, the capacity for wonder and mystery of beginner's mind. It will keep your feet on a genuinely spiritual path.

{three}

PRAYING IN THE NAME OF JESUS

Very truly, I tell you,
if you ask anything of the Father in my name,
he will give it to you.
Until now you have not asked for anything in my name.
Ask and you will receive, so that your joy may be complete.
—John 16:23b-24

From the earliest days, Christians have prayed in the name of Jesus, largely because of the promise, repeated some six times in the Gospel of John, that whatever we ask for in the name of Jesus will be given to us. Day after day, from all corners of the globe, millions upon millions of prayers ascend to heaven punctuated with the words, "in the name of Jesus."

Some of these are simple prayers of praise and gratitude; prayers not expecting an answer; prayers that are meant only to express the faith and feeling of the one praying; pure prayers that give voice to a fundamental affirmation of life. They are, if you will, songs of trust and thanksgiving to the creator of life, sung by hearts that are open to wonder and mystery.

Given the state of humankind, however, I suspect that most of the prayers ascending each day to heaven are, in one way or another, prayers of desperation and need. As Henry David Thoreau, the hermit of Walden Pond, once noted: "Most [people] lead lives of quiet desperation and go to the grave with the song still in them."

So we pray "in the name of Jesus." And yet, if my own experience and my conversations over thirty-three years with others who pray are any measure, many if not most of these millions of prayers "in the name of Jesus" *seem* to go unanswered. Many if not most who pray "in the name of Jesus" seem to experience what the ancient Hebrew poet was experiencing when he or she prayed: "O my God, I cry by day, but you do not answer; and by night, but find no rest" (Psalm 22:2).

Of course, the fact that a prayer is not answered *in the way* that the one who prayed it hoped to have it answered does not mean that it wasn't heard and answered. When they were younger, my kids would "pray" to have pizza for supper every day. They didn't get it. That doesn't mean their "prayer" wasn't heard. It was heard, and the answer was no. Disappointing, to be sure and, from their limited perspective, they were sure that I had not heard their "prayer" at all.

When our prayers seem to be answered only by silence, it just might be that the silence is a divine "No" or "Not yet" or "I have something else in mind." Part of learning to pray is learning to discern answers to prayer with the confidence that in one way or another, prayer is always answered. That great Love that created and sustains the universe and all within it is attentive and responsive to prayer from the beloved. And love, as we shall see, is the key to prayer.

"WHATEVER YOU ASK IN MY NAME"

It is a magical misunderstanding to think that tacking the words "in the name of Jesus" onto the end of a prayer increases its efficacy. It doesn't. Praying in the name of Jesus has no more magical power than does a baseball player making the sign of the cross before facing the first pitch. The name of Jesus is not a talisman by which desires are satisfied and the otherwise unobtainable obtained. Prayer does not work that way.

We should not be wondering if the name of Jesus has magical power; we should be wondering what the name of Jesus *stands for*. What did Jesus stand for, and what did Jesus stand against? What did Jesus call his followers to stand for and against? If Jesus told us to pray for our enemies and do good to those who would harm us, to pray that our enemies would be harmed or even destroyed is not—and can never be—prayer in the name of Jesus.

To pray in the name of Jesus is to pray in ways (and for outcomes) that are consistent with the life and teaching of Jesus. Prayer that is grounded in a concern for justice, for love, for forgiveness, for compassion and mercy, for gentleness and non-violence, for healing and wholeness is prayer in Jesus' name—prayer that transforms both the one who prays and his or her relationships. It sets loose the energies of divine love in ways (and with outcomes) that are often quite surprising.

Many years ago, my daughter came home from a youth activity at church with a rubber bracelet around her wrist, emblazoned with the letters WWJD. What would Jesus do? I thought then, and still do, that wondering WWJD is a good practice not only for young people, but for adults of all ages as well. Spend time deliberately wondering what Jesus would do in the circumstances and relationships that fill your days and you will have a pretty good idea of what to pray about.

We are back at the key theme of this little book. Prayer has much more to do with human transformation than it has to do with somehow getting God to pander to human desires, human ambitions, human prejudice, human pride, and human fears. Prayer has to do with the transformation of human consciousness; it involves learning to have within us "the same mind that was in Christ Jesus" (Philippians 2:5). We want our prayers to reflect and our lives to express what mattered to Jesus. We pray in order to join Jesus in *living* the will of God. In his own words:

Not everyone who says to me, "Lord, Lord," will enter the kingdom of heaven, but only the one who does the will of my Father in heaven. On that day many will say to me, "Lord, Lord, did we not prophesy *in your name*, and cast out demons *in your name*, and do many deeds of power *in your name*?" Then I will declare to them, "I never knew you; go away from me, you evildoers." (Matthew 7:21-22, emphasis added)

It is possible to do and pray for many things "in the name of Jesus" that have little if anything to do with who Jesus was, with what he did, with what mattered to him. To prophesy, to cast out demons, to do deeds of power for the sake of self-aggrandizement, ambition, or pride have nothing to do with Jesus. Such prayer reduces the call "Lord, Lord" to empty words with no meaning or power. Prayer that has to do with Jesus is prayer that flows from a life grounded in Jesus.

On the one hand, then, to pray in the name of Jesus is to pray for what mattered to Jesus; it is to pray that things with ourselves and with others would be the way Jesus would want them to be. On the other hand, to pray in the name of Jesus is to pray that *we* would be the way Jesus would want *us* to be. Christian prayer never leaves things to God alone; it always involves the one who prays in bringing about that which is prayed for. To pray for justice and not be just will not advance the cause of justice. To pray for peace and not be a peacemaker will not bring peace. To pray that the hungry be fed and not to share your own bread will not quench the hunger. To pray that the lonely, the sick, the prisoner be comforted and not to visit them is to bring no comfort.

To pray in the name of Jesus is to join our will to the will of God, and so release the energies of divine and human love in making the world right. Prayer, understood rightly, leads to the transformation of human consciousness and the transformation of human action, which is what St. Paul had in mind when he wrote: "And whatever you do, in word or deed, *do everything in the name of the Lord Jesus*, giving thanks to God the Father through him" (Colossians 3:17, emphasis added).

Love—Where Prayer Begins and Ends

If prayer in the name of Jesus is prayer about what mattered to Jesus, then it is important to know what mattered to Jesus. Again, let me suggest that along with this book you should be reading through the Gospels, coming to your own understanding of what mattered to Jesus, and beginning to wonder why and in what ways it should matter to you.

Even a quick reading of the Gospels will lead to the conclusion that what mattered most to Jesus was love. Once, a scribe came to Jesus and asked him: "Which commandment is the first of all?" Jesus answered:

> The first is, "Hear, O Israel: the Lord our God, the Lord is one; you shall love the Lord your God with all your heart, and with all your soul, and with all your mind, and with all your strength." The second is this, "You shall love your neighbor as yourself." There is no other commandment greater than these. (Mark 12:28-31; cf., Matthew 22:34-40; Luke 10:25-28)

And there is no better ground for prayer than love of God and love of the neighbor.

According to the Gospel of John, on the night before he was murdered by the dark powers that stand against love, Jesus told his followers: "I give you a new commandment, that you love one another. Just as I have loved you, you also should love one another. By this everyone will know that you are my disciples, if you have love for one another (John 13:34-35)." The early Christians took Jesus' love commandment to heart. Paul told the Christians at Rome: "Owe no one anything, except to love one another; for the one who loves another has fulfilled the law. . . . Love does no wrong to a neighbor; therefore, love is the fulfilling of the law" (Romans 13:8, 10).

Some years ago, I heard an interesting teaching story about a young man who was on a spiritual quest. He gathered book after book on spirituality and theology, but found many of them difficult to understand. He decided he needed a spiritual guide. He had heard about such a teacher living nearby, a man of deep spiritual wisdom, respected by all. So, the young man packed all his books in a large chest that he dragged behind him to the teacher's door. He eagerly knocked on the door and awaited the teacher's appearance. When the door finally opened, he saw a kindly face peering out at him.

"And what can I do for you?" the teacher asked.

"Teach me," the young man replied. "I am on a spiritual quest. I want to live a truly spiritual life. I want to learn the way of God."

"And how do you think that I can help you?" asked the teacher.

The young man opened his chest and proudly pointed to his many books. "I want you to teach me everything that is in these books!"

The teacher walked over to the chest full of books and, to the young man's surprise, he slammed it shut. "The way of God is this: Love your neighbor as yourself. All the rest is mere commentary. Now, go. Go out among your neighbors and learn what love means."

The way of God as revealed in the life, teaching, and death of Jesus is indeed the way of love. As St. John succinctly put it: "Beloved, let us love one another, because love is from God; everyone who loves is born of God *and knows God*. Whoever does not love does not know God, for God is love" (1 John 4:7-8, emphasis added). Prayer in the name of Jesus is prayer focused through the lens of love. Indeed, St. Paul goes so far as to say that "*the only thing that counts is faith working through love*" (Galatians 5:6b, emphasis added).

I spent many years in Japan, both as a pastor in Japanese congregations and as a professor at the Japan Lutheran Theological College and Seminary. During my six years at the seminary, I taught a Bible study on the Christian idea of love each year to new Christians. We would work our way through the Old Testament and the New Testament, looking carefully at all the texts that had something to say about God's love and about the love that God desires God's people to express in all the places where they live and work and play.

Toward the end of the study we would finally arrive at 1 Corinthians 13, known as the "love chapter." On the night we studied the love chapter, I would not let my students open their Bibles. I asked them to simply listen to me as I read the chapter to them. The chapter begins with three verses about the absolute centrality of love; they affirm that without love nothing religious matters at all. The next four verses define love as that state of being that focuses on and takes great delight in the good of others. The eighth verse declares that, while everything religious comes to an end, "love never ends."

When I arrived at the last verse of the chapter, I would ask my students to fill in the blank. I would read: "And now faith, hope, and love abide, these three; and the greatest of these is. . . ."

I would ask for a show of hands. "How many think the greatest of these is faith?" I would write the number on the blackboard. "How many think the answer is hope? How about love?" Again the answers were noted on the blackboard. And year after year, with surprising consistency, 70-80 percent of those in my class on love said: "The greatest of these is *faith!*"

I'm not sure how much this has to say about my ability as a teacher! It does have something to say about the church's failure to communicate the heart of Jesus' message—the reality of divine love and the imperative of human love.

Of course, these were new Christians who had come to faith through the ministry of a Lutheran church with its strong emphasis on the notion of justification by faith alone (Romans 3:28; 5:1). It is probably not surprising, then, that they so readily gave the "house answer," which was the wrong answer—faith is not the greatest of faith, hope, and love. "The greatest of these is love."

Toward the end of the class, I would show them a picture I had cut out of the *Japan Times,* a Japanese daily newspaper. It was during the Iran-Iraq War in the 1980s, and the picture was of an Iraqi rocket crew standing next to their still smoking rocket launcher with their hands raised to heaven, praising and thanking Allah for the successful completion of their mission. And the mission? According to the caption under the photo, the Iraqi rockets had landed in an Iranian kindergarten and twenty-three children had been killed. All in the name of God. Done by people of faith. This is not to single out Muslims. Christians have done more than their share of violence in the name of God, as have the adherents of every other major religious tradition.

"And the greatest of these is love," not faith. Finally, I would once more read the first three verses of the love chapter:

> If I speak in the tongues of mortals and of angels, *but do not have love*, I am a noisy gong or a clanging cymbal. And if I have prophetic powers, and understand all mysteries and all knowledge, and *if I have all faith*, so as to remove mountains, *but do not have love*, I am nothing. If I give away all my possessions, and if I hand over my body so that I may boast, *but do not have love*, I gain nothing. (1 Corinthians 13:1-3, emphasis added.)

"If I have all faith . . . but do not have love, I am nothing." Could St. Paul be any clearer? Love is the very content of faith—we believe in love or we believe in nothing. Indeed, faith without love is the most dangerous thing ever loosed upon the earth.

Again, to pray to God in the name of Jesus is to have one's prayer focused sharply through the lens of love. It is to pray for nothing but good for others, even for one's enemies. To pray to God in the name of Jesus is to surrender to the transforming work of the Holy Spirit who would transform us into Christ-likeness, into the very image of love (1 Corinthians 3:17-18). To pray to God in the name of Jesus is to be willing to have God's love perfected in us (1 John 4:12).

In other words, prayer in the name of Jesus won't win you the lottery unless, perhaps, you truly intend to give it all away!

Love is the all encompassing center of Jesus' life and teaching. It is the key to interpreting his teaching, his stories, his actions. Whenever we pray "in the name of Jesus" we need to question whether and in what way our prayer has to do with love.

Love has many constituent elements: justice, mercy, compassion, kindness, generosity, freedom, to name but a few of the key elements of love. As components of love, each is characteristic of Jesus' life and teaching, and provide a lens through which to focus our prayer in the name of Jesus.

Justice

Immediately after his baptism, Jesus went off into the wilderness under the guidance of the Holy Spirit to spend time pondering the will of God and confronting the temptations that are common to humankind: the temptation to give absolute value to material comfort; the temptation to grasp for political, economic, military, and personal power over others to one's own advantage; and the temptation to test rather than trust God (Matthew 4:1-10; Luke 4:1-12).

According to the Gospel of Luke, when he returned from the wilderness, he began to preach in the synagogues of Galilee, teaching about what he had learned of God's will. Eventually he made his way to Nazareth, his hometown, where he went to the synagogue, opened the scroll of the prophet Isaiah, and began to read:

> The Spirit of the Lord is upon me,
> because he has anointed me
> to bring good news to the poor.
> He has sent me to proclaim release to the captives
> and recovery of sight to the blind,
> to let the oppressed go free,
> to proclaim the year of the Lord's favor. (Luke 4:18-19)

When he finished reading, he rolled up the scroll, looked at those silently gathered before him, and declared: "Today this scripture has been fulfilled in your hearing" (Luke 4:21).

The writer of the Gospel of Matthew also quoted from the prophet Isaiah to highlight the fact that Jesus' passion for justice was grounded in God's passion for justice:

Here is my servant, whom I [God] have chosen,
  my beloved, with whom my soul is well pleased.
I will put my Spirit upon him,
  and he will proclaim justice to the Gentiles.
He will not wrangle or cry aloud,
  nor will anyone hear his voice in the streets.
He will not break a bruised reed
  or quench a smoldering wick
until he brings justice to victory.
  And in his name the Gentiles will hope. (Matthew 12:18-21)

From the very beginning of his public career, Jesus declared that (1) justice mattered to God, (2) justice mattered to him, and (3) justice must matter to those who follow him. The biblical idea of justice, of course, has to do with more than a system of criminal and civil law. Indeed, justice as dispensed by the courts may in fact be *unjust* in the light of divine justice. Biblical justice is about fairness, about equity in the distribution of those things that make for a full and rich and meaningful life. To pray in the name of Jesus is to pray that all people get a fair share of food and drink, of shelter, of healthcare, of opportunities for education and meaningful work.

At one point, Jesus roundly criticized religious people for being fastidious with regard to worship and personal piety while at the same time they "neglected the weightier matters of the law: justice and mercy and faith" (Matthew 23:23; Luke 11:42). Here he stands in the tradition of the Hebrew prophets who insisted that the prayers of God's people would not be heard unless they acted justly toward one another (Isaiah 58:1-10), the tradition that declared that the worship of God's people was, in fact, abhorrent to God and would remain so until "justice roll(s) down like waters, and righteousness like an ever-flowing stream" (Amos 5:21-24).

Jesus encourages his followers to pray for justice with passion and urgency, and declares that God will hear such prayer and will grant justice to those "who cry to him day and night" (Luke 18:7).

To pray for justice is to pray in the name of Jesus whose life was grounded in a passion for justice. To pray for justice is to ask God to act in bringing justice to those who suffer from injustice; and it is to express one's own willingness to be someone through whom God acts in bringing justice.

*Set the book down for a moment, and in your journal begin to create a prayer list. Under the heading "**Prayers for Justice**," make three columns. Over the first column write: "**Global and National Concerns**," and then enter in the column instances of injustice in the world and in the United States that you will pray for. Over the second column write: "**Local Concerns**," and then write down instances of injustice in your community that you will pray for. Over the third column write: "**Personal Concerns**," and then jot down any instances of injustice in your personal or work related relationships that you will pray for. Visit this list regularly and use it as a reminder of what to pray for. And remember, to pray is to be willing to act in response to the prayer, trusting that God is acting in and through you. Underneath your list, jot down some suggestions of things you might do with respect to your prayer concerns to help "justice roll down like waters."*

COMPASSION

Another core element of love is compassion, that deep visceral aware-ness of the suffering of others that is accompanied by an equally deep desire to relieve that suffering. Prayer that is driven by compassion is prayer in the name of Jesus. Over and over again in the Gospels, we are told that when Jesus "saw the crowds, he had compassion for them" (Matthew 9:36; Mark 8:2; Luke 7:13).

The Greek word that we translate as compassion literally means to have your bowels twisted in response to someone else's pain; it is that gut-wrenching feeling that we all have had from time to time in the face of another's suffering.

Jesus is the model of true humanity; compassion is a character-istic of the truly human. But we live in a society whose media numbs us to the suffering of others, and whose promotion of self-indulgence encourages indifference to the suffering of others. To pray in the name of Jesus is to wake up, to look around, to see what is really happening in the world. I recently saw a bumper sticker that proclaimed: "If you are not outraged, you're not paying attention." I would change it to read: "If you are not compassionate, you're not paying attention to Jesus." We can all learn to pay attention.

Again, put the book down for a moment and return to your prayer list. Make a list of people you don't know and people you do know for whom you feel compassion. What is it about their circumstances that moves you to compassion? Write down your answers to that question and you will know what to pray about. Don't forget to jot down ideas of what you might do to help relieve the suffering of those for whom you feel compassion.

MERCY AND KINDNESS

According to the Gospel of Matthew, when Jesus began his Sermon on the Mount, he listed several qualities that are characteristic of people who are following him in the way of God; one of them is mercy. "Blessed," he declared, "are the merciful, for they will receive mercy" (Matthew 5:7). In the spiritual calculus of Jesus, what goes around comes around.

Mercy and compassion go hand in hand; mercy is compassionate treatment of those in need, particularly of those over whose lives one's actions have a direct impact. Mercy, as another of the core elements of love, is also a response to Jesus' insistence that his followers be people who forgive; the merciful are inclined toward both kindness and forgiveness. Once when Jesus was roundly criticized by conventional religious folk for eating with (accepting) "tax collectors and sinners," he responded by saying, "Go and learn what this means, 'I desire mercy and not sacrifice'" (Matthew 9:13). Once again, we find Jesus insisting that those things that make for good, healthy relationships, such as mercy, compassion, forgiveness, kindness, and fairness, are infinitely more important than following religious rules, rites, and rituals, if such things get in the way of anyone's wellbeing.

In the well-known parable of the Good Samaritan, Jesus contrasts the mercilessness of two religious leaders—a priest and a Levite—who ignored the plight of a man beaten and left for dead at the side of the road with the mercy of a Samaritan who allowed his own business to be interrupted that he might tend to the needs of the wounded man (Luke 10:25-37).

In the movie *The Four Feathers*, a white, English Christian fighting in a vicious war in Africa is helped, guided, and saved time and time again by a black, African Muslim. Toward the end of the movie, the Englishman asks the African why he, black and Muslim, has risked himself over and over to help him, white and Christian. Showing a profound understanding of true spirituality, the African replied: "Because God put you in my way." Mercy doesn't mind being interrupted by the needs of others. Such interruptions are opportunities for prayer in the name of Jesus.

In the parable of the Unforgiving Servant, Jesus contrasts the mercy of the master who forgives the enormous debt of his servant with that same servant's lack of mercy in refusing to forgive the small debt owed him by another of the master's servants (Matthew 18:21-33). Which is to say that mercy to others is grounded in gratitude to God who is infinitely merciful to us.

Once again, pick up your journal and make a list of your circle of family, friends, coworkers, and acquaintances. Next to each name, jot down the ways in which mercy and kindness from you or from others might relieve their burdens or even give them a new lease on life. There's your list of things to pray for.

MORE CORE ELEMENTS OF LOVE

As you read through the Gospels, you will discover more of the core elements of love simply by paying attention to what Jesus said and what he did. After all, he is love incarnate. You will discover, for example, that Jesus extolled the indiscriminate generosity of God (Matthew 20:1-15; Matthew 5:43-45), and called his followers to emulate that generosity (Matthew 5:48). To pray in the name of Jesus is to pray that the generosity of God would reach all people through the generosity of God's people.

St. Paul had clear insight into the nature of love, not only in 1 Corinthians 13, the "love chapter," but also in Galatians 5:22 where, among the fruit of the Spirit, he listed "joy, peace, patience, kindness, generosity, faithfulness, gentleness, and self-control," all characteristics of those who follow Jesus in the way of God and pray in the name of Jesus.

But take note of this: to be human is to be finite, which means to be limited; it is to be sinful, which means to be self-absorbed and estranged from God and others; and it is to be wounded and broken, our lives damaged and diminished by the cruelties of life. Which is to say that the fruit of Spirit will always be *growing*, never perfected. We are not in competition with others or ourselves to "be spiritual." We should never be tempted to keep a scorecard on how close to perfection we are getting—to do so would be to surrender beginner's mind and become lost in spiritual pride and delusion. Simply do what you can to love and pray in the name of Jesus, which, as we have discovered, means to pray for what Jesus would pray for, and—perhaps without your noticing—the Spirit of God will work within you to cultivate and give gradual growth to the fruit of the Spirit.

Praying for Yourself in the Name of Jesus

It should be clear by now that prayer has as much if not more to do with your relationship to the world God loves than it does to your relationship with yourself. Prayer is not about getting God on your side; it is about moving you to God's side. That does not mean, however, that you should only pray for others and should not pray for yourself.

We will talk more about praying for yourself in chapter five; for now it is enough to point out that, in the concrete situations of your life that call out for love, pray for a loving heart, a loving response, the freedom to act in love. Pray that God would awaken you to the way the world is, give you eyes to see with, and cause compassion to stir in your soul. Pray that justice would be as much a passion for you as it was for Jesus. In each situation, pray for the wisdom to understand what Jesus would do, and pray for the courage to do it. As you move through the day, your joy may be dampened, your peace may be shattered, your patience tried. Depending on what's going on in your day, you may find kindness lacking, generosity stifled, and faithfulness difficult if not impossible. Gentleness and self-control may be beyond you. Pay deliberate attention to yourself. Be mindful of how you are feeling and acting. But don't take off on a guilt trip—that is not the journey you are on. Simply be aware of what's going on for you, and pray in Jesus' name for whatever particular fruit of the Spirit you need in order to be the way you want to be.

Take a moment to add to your growing prayer list concerns for yourself, for your understanding and growth and faithfulness.

{four}

PRAYING JESUS' PRAYER

Pray then in this way:
Our Father in heaven,
hallowed be your name.
Your kingdom come.
Your will be done,
on earth as it is in heaven.
Give us this day our daily bread.
And forgive us our debts,
as we also have forgiven our debtors.
And do not bring us to the time of trial,
but rescue us from the evil one.
—Matthew 6:9-13

Jesus was always going off alone to quiet, solitary places to pray. "He needed time when his attention could be completely on God and on his relationship with God, time to speak and time to listen, time to rest in the love of the one who sent him into the world for love of the world. Clearly Jesus needed the encouragement, the strengthening, the empowerment that comes from encounters with God in deep, intentional times of prayer. If he needed to pray, how much more do we?"[6]

We not only need to pray, we have been hard-wired to pray. There is within us a deep longing to connect to the source of our being, to the One who loved us into existence, a longing to know God and to be known by God. Prayer makes the connection, and answers our yearning for intimacy with God. Jesus knew that.

Jesus' disciples were well aware of Jesus' practice of prayer. They had often seen him go off to pray and had witnessed the comfort, strength, and wisdom that came from his times of solitude with God. They had experienced him as a man of inner peace and equanimity, as a man who came away from prayer knowing who he was and what he was about. It is only natural that they wanted to share the experience.

According to the Gospel of Luke, one day "[Jesus] was praying in a certain place, and after he had finished, one of his disciples said to him, 'Lord, teach us to pray.'" (Luke 11:1). He taught them what has come to be known as the Lord's Prayer. The words of this prayer have been repeated countless times every day for 2000 years and are repeated by billions of Christians every Sunday during worship. Whether or not Jesus intended the prayer to be repeated by rote over and over again, or whether he intended it to teach us *how* to pray and *what* to pray for using our own words is something for scholars to argue over. Prayed with focused attention as Jesus taught it, it is a profound prayer—a prayer that leads us beyond itself to pray with greater specificity about the world we live in, the people we know, the problems we face.

OUR FATHER IN HEAVEN, HALLOWED BE YOUR NAME

"Our Father in heaven." There is something comforting about Jesus' insistence that we address God as a child addresses a parent. The word father (or mother, if the male figures in your life have left you wounded) conjures up images of a loving, caring relationship, one in which the child can trust to be provided for, loved and cared for, and guided in the right direction. To pray to God as a child to a parent expresses both our confidence that God listens to what we have to say and our trust that whatever God asks of us will be good for us. To call God Father or Mother places us within the circle of God's love and care.

But we do not stand within that circle alone. This prayer is to "our" Father, not "my" Father. That little word "our" is very important. Perhaps you have noted that there are no first person singular pronouns in the Lord's Prayer. We never pray this prayer (or any prayer) alone. We always pray in the company of others. If God is "our" Father, then we are part of something larger than ourselves— call it the family of God—and all the people around us are our sisters and brothers, whether they pray this prayer or not.

Whether praying the Lord's Prayer or some other prayer of our own making, we should always be aware of the company we stand in; we should always ponder the impact our prayer might have on the wellbeing of others. It is a powerful experience to feel in your gut the fundamental solidarity you have with all other creatures flung into existence by the exuberance of divine love. To pray "our" Father is to acknowledge our familial relationship to all creatures as well as the mutual responsibility we all have to care for each other.

The movie *Brother Sun, Sister Moon,* a movie about St. Francis of Assisi and his transformation from spoiled son of a wealthy merchant to beggar and fool for Christ, opened my eyes to this familial relationship we have with all creatures. Francis had been gifted with the ability to see God's presence in the simplest of creatures: in birds and animals, in the flowers of the field, and in the poor. Throughout the movie, Francis and his fellow friars referred to common things by calling them brother this or sister that: brother rain and sister mud; brother sun and sister moon; brother stone and sister fire. At first it seemed a bit weird to me, and then I got it: Francis was affirming that there is one God and Father of us all, that all creatures belong to each other, that all creatures are worthy of love for they are the beloved of God. The recognition of God's love for all creatures great and small awoke Francis's heart. Indeed, we are all God's creatures, and if we can come to an experiential understanding of that truth, we will indeed find God's love awakening our hearts as well.

It may indeed seem a bit weird at first, but as you move through your day, if you are captured by something beautiful, send a brief prayer of thanks toward heaven: Thank you God for my sister the flower and brother butterfly; thank you God for brother wolf and sister rabbit; thank you God for brother tree and sister bird; thank you for brother sun and sister moon. And, of course, thank you God for brother Tom and sister Jane and. . . . It is a simple practice, but one you may feel embarrassed to try. Don't be. Use beginner's mind to open yourself to the wonder of all around you, and you will soon discover that your perspective on all around you is changing as God's love awakens your heart.

YOUR KINGDOM COME. YOUR WILL BE DONE ON EARTH AS IT IS IN HEAVEN

The word "kingdom" appears 123 times in the four gospels, 98 times on the lips of Jesus. Clearly the kingdom of God or, alternatively, the kingdom of heaven was at the heart of Jesus' mission. Explaining it, delineating its boundaries in our broken world, and establishing it in and through the lives of his followers mattered to him.

One should not, however, understand the kingdom "geographically," as a place to go. Jesus certainly didn't. Jesus proclaimed that the kingdom was "at hand," breaking into the world in the events of his life and in the faithfulness of his followers. He told his followers that "the kingdom of God is among [and within] you" (Luke 17:21b). Indeed, the Greek word that we translate into English as "kingdom" can (and probably should) be translated as rule or reign.

Whenever people willingly live under the rule of God—which is the rule of love—the kingdom is present. In his *Small Catechism*, Martin Luther declared that God's kingdom is present "whenever our heavenly Father gives us his Holy Spirit, so that through his grace we believe his Holy Word and *live godly lives here in time and hereafter in eternity*."[7] Eternity we can leave in the hands of God—"here in time" our concern is whether or not we are living the best we can under the rule of God. When we pray for the kingdom to come, we pray for the grace to do so. This is certainly prayer "in the name of Jesus."

To pray that God's kingdom come and to pray that God's will be done is to pray the same thing. As we noted in the Introduction, God's will can be profoundly summarized in the words of Micah 6:8: "He [God] has told you, O mortal, what is good; and what does the LORD require of you but to do justice, and to love kindness, and to walk humbly with your God?" Where, and to the degree that, these three happen, the kingdom is present, the rule of God is being followed.

All of which is to say that when we pray for God's kingdom to come and God's will to be done, we are praying that the kingdom come through us, that God's will be done by us. Here is the core of our prayer as we look out on the world we live in: the will of God. What needs to be done in this time, in this place, among these people for God's will to be done, and what's my (our) role in getting it done? The answer to these two questions should end up on your prayer list.

In the Lord's prayer our often petty and self-absorbed, selfish interests are pushed to the side and what God wants for the world takes center stage. Although we say: "*Your* name be hallowed—*Your* kingdom come—*Your* will be done" with our lips, our lives often say: "*My* name, *My* kingdom, *My* will." In the transformation of consciousness that comes from consistent prayer in the name of Jesus, and with beginner's mind, we gradually develop a new perspective on what truly matters and what does not.

GIVE US THIS DAY OUR DAILY BREAD

When Jesus faced those temptations that are common to humankind during his sojourn in the wilderness, the first temptation he confronted was the temptation to turn stone to bread. His response to the temptation was to declare: "One does not live by bread alone, but by every word that comes from the mouth of God" (Matthew 4:4). Pay attention to the fact that Jesus is not advocating either strict asceticism or heroic spirituality. He does not say: "One does not live by bread. . . ." Rather, he says: "One does not live by *bread alone.*" Both matter—bread *and* the Word of God. We are creatures of flesh and blood and need bread. We are creatures of spirit and need the Word.

The word "bread" in Jesus' prayer is clearly a metaphor meaning all the material necessities of life. "In the Hebrew book of Sirach (written about 180 B.C.E.) we are told: 'The necessities of life are water, bread, and clothing, and also a house . . .' (Sirach 29:21). In our globalizing world, we might add to the list: health care, education, the arts, equal opportunity, freedom from political and military violence, in short, whatever gives security, happiness, and meaning to human life. When we pray for daily bread, we pray for it all—for ourselves and for everyone else. No exceptions."[8]

Christian life cannot be reduced to the "spiritual" alone. Praying for and tending to our material needs is every bit as important— indeed, it could be argued that tending to our material needs is every bit as "spiritual" as attending worship and partaking in Holy Communion. After all, the mind-body-spirit connection is so close that care of the one is care of the others. So, add to your prayer list those things that sustain your body and contribute to your overall wellbeing. Just be sure to carefully distinguish between legitimate needs and wants. Although you might never know it from the marketing and entertainment media in our culture, it takes remarkably little to have a rich life full of meaning and joy.

So pray for what you need, but not only for what you need. Pray for what others need as well. Notice that little word "our" again. We pray in Jesus' prayer for "our daily bread." If it is "our" bread, then it is not "my" bread, and no one should have more than enough until everyone has enough.

Take a moment to add to your prayer list the material necessities of life that you could be praying about for yourself. Also make a list of the material necessities you should be praying about for others in your circle of family, friends, co-workers, and acquaintances, as well as in your larger community and in the global village. If there are ways that you can assist in the fair distribution of "bread," make a list of those as well, and pray for the faith and courage to take action.

AND FORGIVE US OUR DEBTS, AS WE ALSO HAVE FORGIVEN OUR DEBTORS

Although Matthew's Greek for what we ask God to forgive us is often translated as "trespasses" or "sins," its literal meaning is debts. As I wrote in my book on the Lord's Prayer:

> It doesn't take a great stretch of the imagination to realize that we are deeply indebted to God. God has created this planet in such a way that it bountifully provides all that is needed for a meaningful and happy life for all people. We are in debt to God in that we have a moral obligation to recognize God's beneficence with the gratitude it deserves. We rarely do. We "owe" God trust and love and a life lived in keeping with God's gracious will—it is a debt that keeps growing as we turn our trust and love towards the things of this world rather than toward the creator of this world.
>
> God deals equitably with us and expects us to deal equitably with each other—our lack of justice is rolled into the debt that we owe God. God has compassion on us and treats us with mercy—our indifference to others adds to the debt that we owe to God.[9]

And so we pray for God to forgive our unpayable debt, *as we also have forgiven our debtors*. What are we owed by others and what do we owe others? St. Paul leaves no room to quibble: "Owe no one anything, except to love one another" (Romans 13:8). If people treat you in ways that are unloving, they are in debt to you. Forgive them as God has forgiven you. If you treat people in unloving ways, you are in debt to them. Seek their forgiveness as you seek God's forgiveness.

If we pray that God would forgive us *as we forgive* others, doesn't that mean that God's forgiveness of us is conditional upon our forgiveness of each other? No. Nothing could be farther from the truth. God's forgiveness is given before it is even asked for and before we could do anything to merit it (for example, see Psalm 103:10-12; Luke 23:34; 2 Corinthians 5:18-19). Why? Because God cares about healthy, hopeful relationships, and without forgiveness such relationships are impossible.

God forgives in order to heal, in order to restore broken relationships, in order to renew hope, and open up a future free from the sins, mistakes, and failures of the past. God's forgiveness is an invitation to make new and better choices (John 8:2-11). We become people who forgive not to earn God's forgiveness, but because the experience of God's forgiveness teaches us that, in a world bounded by sin and brokenness, only forgiveness makes sense. If the cycle of forgiveness does not replace the cycle of violence and retribution, there is no hope. As Mahatma Gandhi reportedly once said, "An eye for an eye makes the whole world blind."

When you pray for forgiveness following Jesus' teaching in the Lord's Prayer, what you are essentially saying is: "God, you keep on forgiving us, and we will keep on forgiving each other, because that's the only thing that makes sense in a world like ours." And then you get down to specifics!

Open your journal again and make a list of the thoughts, attitudes, and actions for which you feel the need for forgiveness from God. Ask for forgiveness and then with a red pen write "forgiven" across the list. Now write down those who are in any way in debt to you, and what they are in debt to you for. With your red pen, write forgiven across the list. Finally, write down the names of those to whom you are in debt, as well as reasons for your indebtedness. Pray for the courage to go to them and ask to be forgiven.

AND DO NOT BRING US TO THE TIME OF TRIAL, BUT RESCUE US FROM THE EVIL ONE

This last petition of the Lord's Prayer highlights the realism of Jesus' understanding of the world we live in. There is no end to the trials, temptations, and testing that men, women, and children face. It is comforting and strengthening, then, to know that:

> No testing has overtaken you that is not common to everyone. God is faithful, and he will not let you be tested beyond your strength, but with the testing he will also provide the way out so that you may be able to endure it. (1 Corinthians 10:13)

And so we pray that we and all others (remember the pronouns "our" and "us") might be saved from times of trial and testing, and be rescued from evil. We will face many different trials in the course of our lives, and so we pray that God's empowering and saving presence might be experienced within them. For example, we will face:

- Moral trials: the temptation to act in unloving, self-centered ways that harm ourselves and others.
- Trials at the hands of others: suffering caused by the unloving, self-centered, and evil acts of others toward us.
- Trials from great loss: suffering and pain from any loss: the loss of a loved one, the loss of an opportunity, the loss of a job, the loss of security, and so forth.
- Trials from illness or injury: the suffering and fear that accompany physical or mental illness or injury.
- Trials from natural disaster: suffering, fear, and dislocation from earthquakes, floods, hurricanes, tornadoes, tsunamis, fire, famine.

The list could on. We are fragile creatures, all too easily harmed, all too easily harming others. And in the experience of being tried, tested, and tempted, it is all too easy to lose heart, to succumb to the lures and enticements of evil, to sink into depression, to give up in the face of seemingly insurmountable odds, suffering, and fear. And so we pray to be saved from the time of trial and to be rescued from evil. We acknowledge our vulnerability, and we ask for the experience of God's presence as a light in the darkness, a rudder in the storm, "a stronghold in times of trouble" (Psalm 9:9).

Take up your journal again and make a list of whatever trials, temptations, or testing you are currently experiencing. Whenever you feel beset, stop and pray for strength, deliverance, rescue. Now make a list of the trials, temptations, or testing confronting your circle of family, friends, coworkers, and acquaintances. There is your prayer list. When you read the news, surf the Internet, or watch television and the temptations, trials, and testing of those in the global village come into your living room, there too is your prayer list. And as always, ponder ways in which your prayer might move you to action.

{five}

WHAT TO DO DURING SET TIMES OF PRAYER

And whenever you pray, do not be like the hypocrites;
for they love to stand and pray in the synagogues and at the
street corners,
so that they may be seen by others.
Truly I tell you, they have received their reward.
But whenever you pray, go into your room and shut the door
and pray to your Father who is in secret;
and your Father who sees in secret will reward you.
—Matthew 6:5-6

In any relationship, intentional time set aside for honest communication is absolutely essential for the relationship to prosper. Prayer is communication. More often than not, prayer is understood as verbal communication, that is, as *telling* God what we have to say about ourselves and others, and *telling* God about our feelings for God. Speaking to God certainly is an important element of prayer, and we will have more to say about that in a moment; however, prayer is much more than simply speaking to God.

Prayer is communication. Think about the many ways in which we communicate with other people with whom we have close and caring relationships:

- We talk to each other.
- We send e-mails and/or letters to the other.
- We read e-mails and/or letters from the other.
- We use our bodies—we smile, we hug, we frown, we turn a cold shoulder.
- We go to special places for conversation: a favorite coffee shop, a walk around the lake.
- We write poetry.
- We sing along with the radio or CD player when the lyrics express our feelings for the other.
- We give gifts that express gratitude and love.
- We make sacrifices for each other.
- We spend time with each other in silence, letting the energy and feelings of love and the experience of intimacy "say" all that needs to be said.

The list could go on; there are so many ways in which we communicate both content and feeling with those we love and care about. Now let's translate this list of the many ways we communicate with others into our prayer life, into our communication with God:

- We talk to God, and we learn to listen for God's speaking in the promptings of our conscience.
- We keep a spiritual journal.
- We study the Bible—the book of what God has to say to us- and read it devotionally.
- We use our bodies: we might assume a certain posture; fold or raise our hands, bow down, make the sign of the cross, meditate while walking.

- We go to special places: we might designate a space for prayer in our home; we might create a home altar; we might visit a hermitage or retreat center once or twice a year; we might find a private spot in the woods, or perhaps beside a river or lake.
- We express our feelings and concerns in art: poetry, music, dance, the graphic arts.
- We sing hymns, chants, and songs of praise.
- We give gifts that express gratitude and love: we might place a flower on our home altar; we give to the poor, the hungry, the disadvantaged, the suffering; we give to our church.
- We make sacrifices for each other: we ponder the sacrifice of Jesus; we meditate on what it means to take up our cross daily and follow him—and we take up the cross.
- We spend time with God in silence: we learn the practice of contemplative prayer or meditation (see chapter seven).

Relationships—whether the relationship between people or the relationship between a person and God—are all about communication. When the communication breaks down, the relationship breaks down. When the communication is good, the relationship is good. As I continue to learn from living with my wife Bobbi, marriage is a way of life whose *primary* focus (not its only focus) is on the relationship two people share. The relationship between a person and God is also a way of life, a way of being in the world that draws all of that person's other relationships into the circle of divine love. That way of life, that way of being in the world is prayer.

Thinking about prayer as a way of life may seem strange to you; for most people prayer is, at best, an add-on to life, something done at the odd moment, on Sunday mornings, or in times of great need or crisis. The notion that prayer is a way of life whose focus is on the relationship between you and God may seem a bit intimidating, if not a bit fanatical. But please, do not be intimidated.

All of the elements of a life of prayer listed above might work for you, and some of them might not, and that is OK. They are offered as suggestions for deepening your relationship with God and moving forward on your journey of faith. Take what works for you and leave what doesn't behind. As you integrate some of these practices into your life, over time other practices might come to seem both possible and meaningful. Start small so you are not overwhelmed. The goal is to develop rhythms of prayer that sustain and strengthen, not to master techniques or tricks of the trade. As you consider various prayer practices, keep beginner's mind. Is this particular practice for you? Maybe so. Maybe not. How will you know? Practice, and then learn from and trust your own experience.

WHEN TO PRAY

You can pray anytime and anywhere, of course, but serious prayer requires the discipline and focus of set times for prayer when, undisturbed and free from distraction, you can do this "work." And it should be approached as work—not work as toil, but work as *vocation,* a serious but joyful expression of who we are.

I suggest a minimum of thirty minutes a day, although in the beginning you might want to start with fifteen or twenty and work your way up to thirty or more. As mentioned in the introduction, although practice doesn't make perfect, it does make progress.

Although you will be spending dedicated time each day in prayer, the content of each session will be different. Variety is indeed the spice of life—including a prayer life. Some days you will work your way through your prayer list; some days you will read the Bible and talk to God about what you find there; other days you will keep a spiritual journal; some days you might write a psalm, compose music, sing hymns. For example, to begin with you might decide to:

- Work through your prayer list on Mondays, Wednesdays, and Fridays.
- Work with the Bible on Tuesdays.
- Work with your spiritual journal on Thursdays.

- Spend time reading from books about prayer and the spiritual life on Saturdays.
- Worship with a community of faith on Sundays.

You will have to craft a schedule that reflects who you are, your interests and abilities, what primary concerns and issues you are facing.

The time of the day doesn't matter. Some people are morning people, and getting up a little earlier than usual while the house is still quiet and the demands of the day are not yet upon you is the best time. Some people are night people, and taking time before bed when the house has settled down, and the day's demands are behind you works best. Depending on the way your life is scheduled, mid-morning or mid-afternoon might work well for you. The time doesn't matter. What matters is taking the time.

I recommend taking the same time each day. It will indicate to you—and to others—the level of seriousness with which you take this "work." It will help you establish a rhythm of prayer as you regularly begin or end the day with time spent alone with God. You will develop a sense of the sacred as the moment for prayer arrives each day at the same time and your awareness shifts to your encounter with the divine.

All this being said, be aware that there will be days when your set time for prayer simply doesn't work. From time to time the exigencies of life cause us to cancel appointments with people we would otherwise love to spend time with. Sometimes we need to cancel our appointments with God. If I call off a lunch with my wife, friend, or co-worker because "something has come up," the relationship is still there, still strong, and there will be other opportunities for lunch. If something comes up and I miss my appointed time of prayer, there will be other times, and my relationship with God is not damaged in any way. In other words, don't approach this work legalistically—seriously, yes, but not so seriously that there is no room for life to interrupt and interfere. Who knows, the interruption might turn out to be more important in your journey of faith than the missed time of prayer.

WHERE TO PRAY

In the same way that it is important to pray at the same time each day, it is important, as much as possible, to pray in the same place. You want to create a space where, when you enter it, your awareness automatically begins to focus on encountering God; a liminal space, as it were, a threshold between ordinary space and sacred space, between ordinary time and sacred time.

If you have both a living room and a family room in your home, you have probably experienced the feeling tone of the two rooms to be different. Enter the living room and the feeling is one of formality; enter the family room and it is one of informality. The living room suggests conversation; the family room suggests fun and video games. A place set aside for prayer suggests centering, intimacy with God, spiritual yearning, an intentional turning toward the will and ways of God. Its feeling tone is one of peacefulness and equanimity; it is a place to feel balanced in an unbalanced world.

Should you be fortunate enough to have a small spare room in your home that can be given over to prayer, furnish it with simplicity in mind: a chair, a small writing desk, a table to be used as a home altar, perhaps a few icons or other pieces of religious art for the walls. On your home altar, you might want to place items of religious significance for you: perhaps a candle, a cross, a vase for flowers, an incense burner, a Bible, a small bowl of water.

If you don't have the luxury of a separate room for prayer, a corner of some other room, say the bedroom or the den, is quite sufficient. Again, you will want something to write on, something to sit on, and a small table for an altar.

As I write this chapter, I am sitting in my small, 12' x 12' office, built onto the back of our detached garage (we have a very small one bedroom house). Every now and then, I glance up from the monitor and look out through a large window at our backyard woods. Behind me is my place for prayer. On the floor is a large cushion; I spent many years as both pastor and professor in Japan, and got in the habit of sitting on the floor and kneeling (with the help of a meditation bench) for prayer. It is a personal thing, I am sure, but I feel more grounded on the floor than I do in a chair—and for prayer, feeling grounded is important. Be that as it may, in front of my cushion, against the wall, is a low wooden table; on the table I have placed a candle, an icon of Jesus, a cross obtained at St. Catherine's Monastery at the base of Mt. Sinai in Egypt, a Tibetan singing bowl (a bell), and three stones that symbolize for me the Holy Trinity. In spring and summer, flowers complete the altar.

I kneel on my cushion at least once and often twice a day; and the very act of kneeling on the cushion, lighting the candle, bowing to the cross, and ringing the bell to signal the beginning of my time at prayer has a deeply centering, focusing effect on me, an effect that carries over into the day when I return to the computer, or cut the grass, or wash dishes, or . . . just about anything.

Of course, you don't need a sacred space to pray; however, I and countless others have discovered that having such a space—especially in the beginning—is a tremendous aid to focusing awareness, to clearing away distractions, and to encouraging the depth of seriousness that prayer requires. Although God is present and can be encountered anywhere, the encounter with God in the microcosm of your own dedicated place for prayer will open and prepare you for the encounter with God in the larger world.

In time you will discover that all space is sacred. According to the book of Exodus, God spoke to Moses from a burning bush. As Moses approached the bush, he was told to take off his shoes because the ground on which he stood was holy ground. With reference to this event, the poet Elizabeth Barrett Browning wrote:

Earth's crammed with heaven,
And every common bush afire with God:
But only he who sees, takes off his shoes,
The rest sit round it and pluck blackberries.[10]

Experiencing a sacred space in your own home each day will, over time, open you to the reality that all ground is indeed holy ground and "every common bush afire with God."

I strongly urge that you create a dedicated space for prayer in your home. You will be following Jesus advice: "But whenever you pray, go into your room and shut the door and pray to your Father who is in secret; and your Father who sees in secret will reward you" (Matthew 6:6). But feel free to move outdoors and find a second place where, surrounded by the mystery and beauty of the natural world, you can pray. I have cut a meditation path through the woods behind my house. At the top of the path, in a grove of birch and poplar, is a bench, and beside the bench a flower stand. It is a quiet and beautiful place for just sitting and communing with God—with or without words.

If you live in a city, it will be more difficult—but not impossible—to find an outdoor place for prayer. It might be as simple as a chair in your backyard or a bench in an out-of-the-way corner of a park. One can find both the beauties of nature and solitude in a city—even with other people in view.

TALKING WITH GOD

Once you have the time set and the place prepared for prayer, what are you going to do at that time and in that place? Many things, depending on the day and depending on what's going on in your life, but perhaps more often than not—especially in the beginning—you are simply going to talk to God, and then listen to the promptings of your conscience for what God might be saying to you.

If you grew up praying the Lord's Prayer in its traditional version, with its thees, thous, and thines, you may think that the language of prayer is the language of the King James Bible—formal, old, archaic, and often difficult to understand. Nothing could be further from the truth. The language of prayer is the language of everyday life.

You talk to God with the same language you talk to your spouse, friends, co-workers, strangers you meet in the grocery store. If you are grateful, you use the language of gratitude; if you are in need, you use the language of asking or pleading; if you are anxious, you use the language of worry or fear; if you are sad, you use the language of sorrow; if you are happy, you use the language of joy. No matter what you are feeling or experiencing, you express it to God in the same language you would express it to another person. If you are angry at God or another person, express your anger in prayer. There is nothing wrong with being angry—even at God. As the writer to the Ephesians put it, "Be angry but do not sin; do not let the sun go down on your anger . . ." (Ephesians 4:26). Being angry is not sin—Jesus was angry from time to time. Staying with the anger, living in the anger, refusing to let go of the anger, acting out of the anger in an attempt to harm the other—that's sin.

So use your ordinary language in prayer; be yourself. What matters is honest speech, being vulnerable, taking the risks of self-disclosure. Prayer is a conversation between lovers, and love always demands honesty, even when it is painful.

Beginning your prayer time

Light your candle, if you have one; ring your bell, if you have one; settle into your chair or onto your cushion; bow reverently to the cross, if you have one; make the sign of the cross if that is a comfortable thing to do; and then tell God how you are feeling at the moment. Are you happy or sad, irritable at having to pray or glad to be there, angry at something (or someone) or at peace with all, engaged or indifferent, feeling up or feeling down? Feelings are what they are—express them and do your best to let them go and get down to the business of prayer. Don't let them become obstacles to prayer. I may be irritated with my wife, but that is no excuse for not talking with her about what needs to be talked about.

You will find it to be part of the focusing and centering process to simply tell God how you are feeling at the moment. Unacknowledged and unexpressed feelings can exert a strongly negative influence on your ability to focus. To simply acknowledge them before God helps to rob them of their power to distract and control you.

Next offer up a prayer for wisdom in knowing what to pray for and how to pray for it. James put it succinctly: "If any of you is lacking in wisdom, ask God, who gives to all generously and ungrudgingly, and it will be given you" (James 1:5). Pray that the Holy Spirit who dwells within you (John 14:15-17) would guide your prayer. Jesus promised that the Spirit would lead us into the truth (John 16:13), and so there is no reason not to pray expectantly. Faith, that is, trust that God is indeed involved in our prayer, both moves us to prayer in the first place, and deepens over time through our own experience.

If there is anything that needs to be confessed, now would be the time to do it. Confess to God anything that you need to confess, and then let it go; it is forgiven. Don't let guilt keep you from the work of prayer. Acknowledge your sins, failures, mistakes, let God know that's not the way you want to be, and then get on with things, trusting that God's unconditional forgiveness has opened a new future for you wherein you can make new and better choices.

Praying for yourself

After reading the last two chapters, you know that I encourage keeping a prayer list—and if you've done the little exercises suggested in the last two chapters, you're well on your way to having a prayer list to begin with.

As you look through your prayer list, you will note that most prayers fit into two categories: (1) prayers for yourself (usually called "petitionary prayer" in churchly jargon), and (2) prayers for others ("intercessory prayer"). For both kinds of prayer, keep in mind what was said in chapter three about praying in the name of Jesus, and then just start telling God what you want and why you want it.

Do not be surprised if over time you find yourself spending less and less time praying for yourself. As you continue on this journey, you will find yourself increasingly entrusting yourself to God's providential care, which means that your prayer will turn more toward the needs of others than your own needs. It happens naturally. Don't worry about it and don't try to force it. If you are beginning in prayer, just pray for whatever you think you need for yourself.

Rather quickly, you will find yourself praying less and less about your material needs, and more and more about your psychological and spiritual needs. Within the relationships and context of your life, do you find yourself needing wisdom, discernment, understanding? Pray for it. Do you find yourself needing to develop patience? Pray for it. Do you need skills in anger management? That's a topic for conversation with God. Do you need to know more of what love means in a particular relationship or circumstance? Talk to God about it. Having trouble forgiving or asking for forgiveness? Work the problem through with God. Feeling like you could use a bigger harvest of the fruit of the Spirit (Galatians 5:22)? Pray about it.

Just be sure that these prayers are hopeful. There are two things to keep in mind as you pray for emotional/psychological and spiritual growth. First, you are a work in progress. As we mentioned earlier, the Spirit of Christ is within you working to transform you more and more into the likeness of Christ (1 Corinthians 3:17-18). Your job is simply to be willing to take the journey of transformation, wherever it may lead. No guilt over failures. No pride over accomplishments. Beginner's mind, not expert's mind. This is a journey of learning, of growth, of exploration.

Second, be gentle with yourself. Gentleness is a fruit of the Spirit. As you continue in prayer, as your awareness of the divine presence all around you deepens, you will begin to look at all around you with more and more gentleness. You will see the fragility and vulnerability and preciousness of all life, and will grow in the ability to accept and forgive. As I mentioned above, spiritual growth happens naturally as you surrender to the life-transforming power of the Holy Spirit; to attempt to force it is to impede it. Just be sure, when you begin to experience an impulse towards gentleness in the relationships and circumstances of your life, to turn the focus of that gentleness on yourself as well. Acknowledge your own fragility, vulnerability and preciousness, and be accepting and forgiving of yourself.

Praying the prayers of others as prayers for yourself

As you read the Bible and other spiritual writing, from time to time you will find prayers that resonate with you, prayers that speak the yearning of your own soul. Copy them into your journal and, when the occasion is right, pray them during your set time of prayer. I have copied several over the years. In the Bible, you will find the book of Psalms a profound source of prayers that might well touch your heart and speak your longing. Take a look at Psalm 63:1-8, Psalm 42:1-2, Psalm 51:1-12, and Psalm 139:1-18, 23-24.

In times of great trial, Jesus' prayer on the night he was betrayed into the hands of those who would kill him might well prove a source of comfort, strength, and determination for you: "Father, if you are willing, remove this cup from me; yet, not my will but yours be done" (Luke 22:42). As you read through the Bible, keep on the lookout for words that speak your heart to God, and make them your prayers.

The prayers of others on the spiritual journey may also resonate deeply with your own experience. I have long made the prayer commonly attributed to St. Francis of Assisi my prayer:

Lord, make me an instrument of your peace;
where there is hatred, let me sow love;
where there is injury, pardon;
where there is doubt, faith;
where there is despair, hope;
where there is darkness, light;
and where there is sadness, joy.
O Divine Master,
grant that I may not so much seek to be consoled as to console;
to be understood, as to understand;
to be loved, as to love;
for it is in giving that we receive,
it is in pardoning that we are pardoned,
and it is in dying that we are born to Eternal Life. Amen.

To pray this prayer is certainly to pray in the name of Jesus. When you find prayers like this, from either the Bible or the work of some spiritual writer, I suggest that you memorize them so they are there for you at the moment you need them, and so that the power of their words takes residence in your consciousness.

One prayer that I discovered years ago, shortly after graduating from seminary, said exactly what I was feeling then, and have felt many times since:

My Lord God, I have no idea where I am going. I do not see the road ahead of me. I cannot know for certain where it will end. Nor do I really know myself, and the fact that I think that I am following your will does not mean that I am actually doing so. But I believe that the desire to please you does in fact please you. And I hope I have that desire in all that I am doing. I hope that I will never do anything apart from that desire. And I know that if I do this you will lead me by the right road, though I may know nothing about it. Therefore I will trust you though I may seem to be lost and in the shadow of death. I will not fear for you are ever with me, and you will never leave me to face my perils alone. Amen.[11]

This prayer from the experience of Thomas Merton might well speak to someone who prays with beginner's mind. It reflects openness in the face of uncertainty, a willingness not to know all the answers, and a fundamental trust that God is present, even in the ambiguities of life, and so "all will be well, all will be well, all manner of things will be well."[12]

To take the prayers of others and make them your own is not spiritual laziness if, that is, they connect with your own experience, express your own desires, and give you a sense of connection and solidarity with others who have taken—or are taking—the same journey you are.

Praying for others

Christian faith is not individualistic. It is never only about me. We always stand before God as part of both the community of faith and the larger community of humankind. Christian faith connects us to everyone. When anyone suffers, we all suffer, when things go well for anyone, things go well for everyone. As the seventeenth-century English poet John Donne so beautifully put it:

Any man's death diminishes me
because I am involved in mankind. . . .[13]

To be Christian is to be involved in humankind from the vantage point of love. As we saw in chapter three, Christian faith and life are driven by a passion for justice grounded in Jesus' passion for justice. Compassion and mercy, driven by an acknowledgement of our common fragility, vulnerability, and preciousness, move us to prayer and action on behalf of others.

When praying for others, the tendency is to be as specific as possible, which usually means asking God for specific outcomes. This could cause spiritual blindness. When you are looking for specific outcomes, it is not unusual to assume that God is either silent or absent when those outcomes aren't delivered, even though the answer to your prayer might be staring you in the face.

I have a friend who loves vegetables in general, but had her heart set on asparagus in particular to accompany the pasta dish she was planning for dinner. She went to the local market and headed straight for the produce section where she searched and searched for asparagus to no avail. There was none. She left disappointed and empty-handed, never noticing, in her fixation on asparagus, the prominent display, right in front of her, of beautiful, fresh green beans. She had no green vegetable with her pasta that night. Perhaps she should have been a little less specific and open to more possibilities than asparagus! In other words, it might be better to pray for others in more general terms rather than in specific terms, and stay open to the myriad of ways in which God may be active in the life of the person you are praying for.

If Emma is grieving the loss of her husband, rather than pray that she would join the quilting club at church so she can "work out her grief in the company of friends," it might be best simply to ask God to bring her comfort, and to meet her needs, whatever they are. And to let God know that you will "be there" for her in whatever ways compassion suggests.

I began thinking this way when I was the academic dean at Luther Seminary in St. Paul, Minnesota. During a chapel sermon, Professor Arland Hultgren said something quite profound, that has stayed with me ever since. "Never," he said, "presume to understand another's suffering or need." More often than not, we do not (and cannot) know with any specificity what other people are experiencing, what the shape and substance of their pain is, what they truly need to move toward wellbeing. To pray as if we did can all too easily result in our taking a judgmental and prideful stance against them—attitudes that should never enter the time of prayer.

Praying for others in their need is to humbly commit them into the hands of God who understands their need far better than we do or can. To pray for others is both to trust God for the solution to their need, and to be willing to be part of the solution. To pray for others is simply to love them, and to be willing to be there for them and with them.

When praying for others, there is a tendency to focus on their needs, their problems, their suffering. Important as that is, life is about far more than needs, problems, and suffering. St. Paul tells us to "weep with those who weep," but also—and just as important-ly—to "rejoice with those who rejoice" (Romans 12:15). If Kathryn and Tim are celebrating their fiftieth wedding anniversary, you might thank God for their life together and ask God to give them more good years of delight in each other. If Amy just got a new job, you might thank God for the new opportunity and the excitement she is feeling, and ask God to be with her in the transition she faces.

When you read through your prayer list, pay attention to how many of the things you are praying for fit in the category of weeping with those who weep, and how many fit in the category of rejoicing with those who rejoice. If there is not a pretty good balance between them, chances are you are paying more attention to the harshness of life than to the goodness of life. Such an imbalance in your prayer list may point to an imbalance in your life. Be real about those things where weeping is called for, but look as well for those things that call for rejoicing.

When you pray for others, to the degree that it is possible, let them know you are praying. Tell Emma that you are praying for her in her grief, and asking God to comfort her in her sorrow. Let Kathryn and Tim know you thanked God for their life together, and are praying that God sustain them in their joy. Tell Amy you thanked God for her new job, and are praying that she experience God's presence in this new environment. When you let people know you are praying for them, you strengthen and encourage them—a goal of prayer—and in the conversation you might discern ways in which you can be helpful to them—another goal of prayer.

PRAYING FOR HEALING

I have been in a lot of hospital rooms over the years. I've talked with people of all ages and listened as they shared their anxiety and sometimes fear and sometimes anger over what was going on with them. I've prayed with them, tried to walk with them through the experience of serious illness or injury, and often just sat in silence with them, sometimes holding their hand. And sometimes I've been in the room when they died.

I remember one such time, and it was not a good death. The man was angry and afraid. He had been angry and afraid much of his life. He was angry at God because his life had not gone the way he had hoped, and he attributed this in part to God not answering his prayers in the way he wanted. He was angry at others, in particular his parents and his wife, for not being there for him the way he wanted them to be. His anger crystallized when he discovered he was dying of cancer. He blamed God for not making him well; he blamed me for failing to pray well enough to convince God to make him well; he blamed his wife and parents for not understanding his suffering, for not being sympathetic enough. And he was afraid; afraid of the God he was angry at; afraid of dying. No matter how much I and others talked with him, sat with him, and tried in every way to be there with and for him, he couldn't let go of his anger or his fear. As death approached, his terror grew. Finally he slipped into a coma from which he never awoke.

Through that and other experiences, I have come to distinguish between a "cure" and a "healing." A cure is when you get physically well. Your body mends from an injury, you recover from your illness. You go back to life pretty much as it was before the illness or injury.

I always pray for a cure, and I let the people I'm praying for know that I am praying for a cure. I have seen times when against all medical hope people have seemed "miraculously" cured. I have seen times when the body—with the help of modern medicine and skilled medical practitioners—cured itself. And there is no reason not to think that God is involved in such cures—after all, God created the human body with natural capacities to recover from illness and injury. I have seen times when the cure is partial; cancer goes into remission, heart disease is held at bay with bypass surgery, AIDS kept under control. And I have seen times when there is no cure and the patient dies. I always pray for a cure.

But I also pray for healing. You are healed when your mind and spirit are at peace with what's happening to your body. So much illness and injury are accompanied by mental and spiritual anguish, by fear, by anger and bitterness, by loneliness, by confusion, by religious doubt and despair, by a strong resistance to accepting and coming to terms with what's going on with you. Healing comes with an acceptance of what's happening, and the trust that even if I die, yet shall I live (John 11:25-26). When healing has happened, people are at peace with themselves, with their family and friends, and with God.

Over the years, I have seen:

- People who have been cured but not healed. They left the hospital or the sickroom physically restored, but still emotionally, mentally, and spiritually distressed.
- People, like the man I mentioned earlier, who have not been cured, and have not been healed. This is a bad death.
- People who have not been cured, but have been healed. They may remain ill or they may die, but now they face their continuing illness or their death in the company of those who love them, with an acceptance grounded in trust that their lives are kept safe in the love of the God who made them. When they die, it is a good death.
- People who have been both cured and healed. This is wonderful.
- People who were healed long before illness or injury struck; people who live so close to God in mutual love that they are able, like St. Paul, to be content in all things.

Of course, there will come a time when no amount of prayer will bring a cure. Human mortality is 100 percent. We will all pass through the gates of death. It is good, then, to pray for both ourselves and others that when the time comes to die, we will have a good death.

So pray for those who are ill or injured. Pray for a cure and pray for healing, and let them know you are praying. Pray during your fixed time of prayer, and pray when you are with them, even if your prayer consists of words spoken in the silence of your own heart while you hold their hand.

And don't wait for illness or injury to strike to pray for healing. To one degree or another, we are all wounded in mind and spirit. To one degree or another, we are all anxious and fearful, estranged from one another and from God. To the extent that we are aware of our own or others' emotional, mental, and spiritual distress and disease, we should pray for the healing power of God's Holy Spirit, that we all might have a good life and a good death.

MANAGING YOUR PRAYER LIST

You can keep your prayer list in your journal or in another notebook. For ease of use, I suggest a separate notebook, small enough to carry with you. Keep two lists. If you are using a separate notebook, start the first list on the first page and the second list about halfway through the notebook. That will give both lists space to grow. Label one list "Prayers for myself," and the other "Prayers for others."

For each entry, briefly write what you are praying for. To make it easy to keep an eye on balance, write prayers of "weeping" using a red pen, and prayers of "rejoicing" in blue or black. Leave several inches of blank space between each entry. When you are done praying, look over your list. In the blank space beneath each entry, jot down what your conscience might be suggesting about what *you* could do to respond to your prayer. Are there any ways in which the community of faith might act in this particular situation? Jot it down. Should you or the community of faith take some action, note in this space what happened as a result. Any new actions suggested? Write them down.

Look for signs of God's presence in the situation you are praying about. Write them down. Do you discern that your prayer has been (or is being) answered? Write it down. Keep a concern on your prayer list as long as you think there is good reason to keep on praying. Check in from time to time with the people you are praying for. If you think the situation you are praying about has been resolved, then remove the concern from your list.

Every so often, say once every month or so, read through your prayer list and study the notes you have been taking. It is a way of schooling yourself in the ways of God and of God's people, and it will help sensitize you to the presence of God in your life and in the lives of those for whom you pray.

USING YOUR BODY IN PRAYER

We are a unity of mind, body, and spirit, and should engage our bodies, as well as our minds and spirits, in the practice of prayer. Simple movements, postures, or gestures can have profound symbolic meaning, and leave us feeling more integrated and whole. Using the body in prayer is personal, and what is meaningful for some will not be meaningful for others. Here is a smorgasbord of suggestions for you to sample and see what works for you:

- As a sign of reverence, bow your head briefly before your home altar before settling onto your chair or cushion.
- Make the sign of the cross as you begin (and end) your prayer as a sign that you are a follower of Jesus. (Place the fingers of your right hand on your forehead, then lower them to your chest, move them to your left shoulder, to your right shoulder, then back to your chest in one fluid movement.)
- Keep a small bowl of fresh water in your prayer space. As you enter, dip your fingers in the water and mark a small cross on your forehead in remembrance of your baptism.
- Genuflect as a sign of reverence (bend and touch one knee to the floor) as you enter and leave your prayer space.
- Kneel while you pray.
- Stand while you pray.
- Sit while you pray, but keep your feet flat on the floor and back straight in an attitude of reverent alertness.
- Fold your hands.
- Raise your arms, palms up.
- Rest your hands in your lap, palms up.
- Strike a bell to signal the beginning of your prayer, and again to signal the end of your prayer.
- In order to calm body, mind, and spirit before prayer, do a few slow stretching exercises or Yoga postures.

You will have to determine what is meaningful for you. Don't force yourself to do things that feel empty or uncomfortable, but recognize that you will have to try these movements, postures, and gestures several times before knowing from *experience* whether or not they are an aid to prayer for you.

READING

If communication is a two-way street, then one should be as concerned with listening as with speaking. We have already mentioned that listening to the promptings of our conscience is one important way of discerning what God is saying to us. Another way is reading the Bible. The two are connected. The more we live in the Bible, the more likely we are to pick up on what God is saying in the promptings of our conscience in particular situations.

At least once a week you should give your fixed time of prayer over to reading the Bible. And you should read with a notebook by your side. As you read, write down key insights, new ideas, questions, doubts, ideas to pursue, things you might want to ask your pastor about, any changes in attitude or behavior suggested by the text. If the text suggests things you should be praying about, stop for a moment, add the concern to your prayer list, pray, and go back to reading. Keep asking yourself: "What does God have to say to me in the text I'm reading? What does God have to say to my community of faith?" If prayer is understood as communication, then reading the Bible with these questions in mind is every bit as much "prayer" as talking to God is.

I recommend that you read from a study Bible, that is, a Bible that has introductions to each book of the Bible, footnotes explaining historical content and theological ideas, cross-references to related biblical texts, a glossary of biblical terms, a concordance (an alphabetical listing of key words in the Bible showing where they can be found in both Old and New Testaments), and maps of the biblical world. The Bible was written in historical, geographical, and social/economic/political contexts vastly different from our own. These study helps will assist you in "entering" the world of the Bible and those who wrote, read, and listened to it. They will make the Bible more accessible and understandable, far more interesting, and more helpful in discerning what God is saying to us today in our hugely different world.

There are many different translations of the Bible available in bookstores. I usually recommend, in order of personal preference: (1) the New Revised Standard Version (NRSV) and (2) the New Jerusalem Bible (NJB). Browse in a bookstore to find a Bible whose study helps seem to you to be easy to navigate. With respect to the NRSV, I use the Oxford Annotated Bible. For the NJB, take a look at the Doubleday Standard Edition published in 1999.

As you continue walking the path of prayer, you might find yourself becoming more and more interested in the Bible, its world, its thought, its faith. If so, consider exploring the wealth of information to be found in biblical commentaries, works by biblical scholars on individual books of the Bible. In the suggestions for further reading at the back of the book, I will recommend commentaries that are accessible to ordinary readers. But remember, the goal is not to become an "expert" on the Bible, it is to learn to hear God speaking to you today through these ancient words. You need not be a scholar to catch the divine voice.

Prayerful reading of the Bible is reading that expands your consciousness of God and your awareness of God's presence in the ordinariness of everyday life. When reading the Bible in a prayerful way, read slowly, savor each word, sentence, paragraph. Let each word have its own moment in your consciousness, a moment to suggest associations, to evoke insights, to raise questions. Be like the prophet Jeremiah who (metaphorically, of course) declared to God: "Your words were found, and I ate them, and your words became to me a joy and the delight of my heart . . ." (15:16).

And remember to keep beginner's mind. In response to a new insight or an old conclusion, ask yourself: "Is this what God is saying to me? Maybe so. Maybe not so." Test your insight or conclusion in the crucible of your own experience—live it, talk to other people of faith about it, see where it takes you, keep reading, keep praying. Such is the path you are walking.

Along with the Bible, it is good to spend some time reading what others have to say about the spiritual life. Shortly before graduating from the seminary, I discovered the work of Thomas Merton, one of the most important spiritual thinkers and writers of the last century. Through his work, Merton became my teacher. I couldn't count the number of books on prayer, meditation, and spirituality that I have read in the last thirty-three years. I have learned much and, in the process, connected my own experience of seeking and encountering God with the experience of countless others. You will find a few suggestions for spiritual reading in the back of the book. I am sure you will discover, as I did, that each book read suggests another, and before you know it, your bookshelves will be as crowded as mine.

KEEPING A SPIRITUAL JOURNAL

The first time I traveled overseas I bought two notebooks, a large spiral notebook and a smaller notebook that fit in my shirt pocket. The larger notebook was a journal of my journey; I wrote in it every night before calling it a day. The smaller one went with me throughout the day, a place to make quick jottings about the places, people, and happenings of the day—memory jogs for the journal writing I would do in the evenings.

It was, and continued to be, a fascinating experience. As my good friend Ron Klug wrote in his excellent book, *How To Keep A Spiritual Journal:*

> A journal is . . . a tool for self-discovery, an aid to concentration, a mirror for the soul, a place to generate and capture ideas, a safety valve for the emotions, a training ground for the writer, and a good friend and confidant.[14]

My journal, on that first overseas trip (which ended up lasting sixteen years!) was all that and more. Along with being a "tool for self-discovery," it became a tool for discovering God. Along with being a "mirror for the soul," it became an avenue through which my soul learned to communicate—to speak and to listen—to God. My journal was a book of prayer.

I wish I had had a book like Ron Klug's to guide me. My development as a journal writer was a pretty hit and miss thing. I just did it, and it developed. At first, my journal was pretty much a chronicling of the places I went, the people I met, and the things I did during the day—what Klug calls "a daybook, a place to record daily happenings." In time, my journal writing expanded to include:

- My feelings about those daily happenings, the places I went, the people I interacted with.
- My questions about them.
- Insights as to who and how I am that emerged from the events and interactions of the day.
- Musings about the relationship between the events and interactions of the day and my faith.
- Ponderings on where and how God was present in the day, and where God seemed absent or silent during the day.
- Thoughts on how the events and interactions of the day either affirmed or challenged my faith.
- Key insights/ideas/questions arising from Bible readings or other spiritual readings.
- A daily meditation on: "What (if anything) do I think God was saying to me today?"
- Poetry expressing my relationship to creation and creation's Creator.

My journal did indeed become a friend and confidant, and a companion on the journey of awakening to God and myself.

So, grab yourself two notebooks—a large one and a small one—and start engaging your own journey of awakening to God and yourself through the powerful and healing practice of journaling. You may want to journal during your regular daily time of prayer, or you may want to add another time of prayer each day just for journaling. Praying in the morning and journaling in the evening is a wonderful way to bookend the day.

When you journal, you are writing for yourself and God alone, so be honest, even if it is something you might be embarrassed about should another person know what you are writing. Just safeguard your journal. Don't worry about proper punctuation, correct grammar, or apt word selection—you're not writing for publication, you're writing to know yourself, your world, and your God better. So just write. And at the end of each month, go back and read everything you've written. It will help you discover the ways in which you are the author of your life and the ways in which God is the Author of your life.

SPENDING TIME IN A HERMITAGE OR RETREAT CENTER

According to the Gospels of Matthew, Mark, and Luke, in the beginning of his public career, Jesus went off to the wilderness to spend time alone contemplating both the will of God and the ways of the world, and preparing himself to follow the way of God in his return to the world. When he came out of the wilderness, he plunged into the world of human sorrows and joys and began to teach and heal.

The wilderness is a place away from the distractions of daily life, a place where life is reduced to the necessary and the simple, where there is nothing to fill the silence where God speaks (1 Kings 19:11-12). Which is to say that getting away from time to time is important.

In 1980, some five years after beginning the serious practice of prayer, I took my first trip to the "wilderness," a three-day retreat at a Jesuit monastery in Lake Elmo, Minnesota. It was a silent retreat. There were about twenty of us, and we were asked not to speak to each other for the duration of the retreat. During mealtimes we would sit together around large round tables, but we kept silent. It is amazing how close to others you can begin to feel without ever speaking to them, but by simply sharing a meal while listening to a Jesuit brother read aloud from a spiritual classic.

Each day was bookended with worship. The singing of the liturgy and the hymns was the only time words escaped our lips. For one hour each morning and one hour each afternoon we came together for a conference, a talk by the retreat master on the practices of the spiritual life. For the rest of the day we were free to wander the grounds, to sit in the library or our own sleeping rooms, to reflect on what we had been taught, to pray, to meditate, to journal. No distractions, just the experience (strange at the time) of being alone with myself and God. I left the retreat center on Sunday afternoon with a rather remarkable feeling of peace and equanimity, along with the determination to do it again. I also left with a deeper sense of connection to the God in whom "we live and move and have our being" (Acts 17:28).

Since then, I have gone into the "wilderness" at least once and often twice a year. Early on, I would attend silent retreats with others; we would learn and pray together, learn and pray alone. In 1994, I discovered a place called *Pacem in Terris* (Peace on Earth), a retreat center in St. Francis, Minnesota, that has some fifteen or sixteen hermitages spread out in the woods, small cabins designed for completely private retreats. A week spent in the solitude of a hermitage each fall and each spring, with nothing to do but pray, read, reflect, and journal, has proven a gift beyond measure. These sojourns in the "wilderness" have given me much food for the journey. And they will for you as well.

To begin with, I encourage you to find a place where you can retreat with other people, a place where prayer and meditation and the dynamics of Christian spirituality are taught, and where you are given plenty of time for reflection and practice.

In time, you might well begin to experience the desire for greater solitude rising within you. That would be a sign that it is time to try a private retreat—anywhere from three days to a week—in a hermitage or retreat center that supports private retreats.

Your pastor will likely be able to recommend places for you to spend time in the "wilderness." Or you could Google "Christian retreat center," or "Christian retreat house," or "Christian hermitage" along with your state's name.

When you have come out of the "wilderness" and returned home after your retreat, be sure to debrief with your pastor or a spiritual friend. It will help you evaluate and integrate your retreat experience so that the fruit of your experience continues to grow in the days, weeks and months ahead.

A CONCLUDING WORD ON FIXED TIMES OF PRAYER

Praying in the morning, journaling in the evening, taking a week on retreat each spring and fall can sound a bit daunting in the beginning. In a very short time, however, having such fixed times for prayer will be as natural as having fixed times for eating, for sleeping, for working, for recreating. They will work themselves into the rhythms of your life, and one day you will suddenly become aware that prayer is not something that you do—it's who you are.

six

PRAYER ON THE RUN

Rejoice always,
pray without ceasing,
give thanks in all circumstances;
for this is the will of God in Christ Jesus for you.
—1 Thessalonians 5:16-18

It is amazing to walk in any public place where people hurry to fro and take notice of how many are on a cell phone, either talking or texting. Billions of e-mails race through the ether on any given day, often snatched out of the ether on BlackBerries or other portable devices. We are a people on the run and a people who constantly communicate on the run with others who are important to us.

Just thirty seconds ago I received a phone call from my wife, standing in Target with a question she wanted to ask me. Earlier, before heading off to Target, she called me from the parking lot of the clinic where she had just had a routine annual physical, just checking in to let me know how things had gone. We are not unusual. When our kids come to visit, they are never more than a foot away from their cell phones and BlackBerries. Wherever you go one of the most common sights is that of people of all ages walking with their heads down, staring at the small glowing screen in their hands. Throughout the day, we stay connected with family, friends, co-workers, clients.

And so it should be in our relationship with God. For people who give themselves over to the discipline of daily prayer at a fixed time in a fixed place, communicating with God on the run comes naturally. When Christians don't practice such prayer, however, they often end up leading somewhat schizophrenic lives. On Sunday they worship, confess their faith, connect with the sacred; on Monday through Saturday they live their lives with little if any reference to the God they worshiped on Sunday. The workplace, marketplace, and playground are experienced as secular places where religious concerns seem to have little relevance.

Those who practice daily prayer in the sanctuary of their homes, however, soon come to see and experience that God is everywhere present, everywhere to be encountered, everywhere to be talked to and listened to. God cannot be contained in the church or in our fixed times and places of prayer. Paradoxically, God is both "out there" and "within" us. In an even more profound and paradoxical sense, we are "within God," for God is the one "in whom we live and move and have our being" (Acts 17:28). As Jesus told his followers, "On that day you will know that I am in my Father, and *you in me, and I in you*" (John 14:20, emphasis added).

Regular prayer leads to an ever deeper experience of our union and communion with God, a communion that does not stop when we leave the place of prayer and enter the larger world of work, relationships, and play. Praying on the run, opening to God in the events and relationships that fill our days, is to experience the transforming, enlivening power of the Spirit of Jesus in the ordinary moments where life is ordinarily lived.

Praying on the Run for Those on Your Prayer List

From time to time during your day, you will most likely run into someone who is on your prayer list, or something will happen to bring them to mind. When that happens, take a moment to mentally embrace them with the love of God that is within you.

St. John declared: "No one has ever seen God; if we love one another, God lives in us, and his love is perfected in us" (1 John 4:12). Which is another way to say that prayer perfects God's love within the one who prays, and communicates God's love to the one who is prayed for. Prayer for another is a deep act of love, and in that act of love God's love is present and powerful.

So when you run into or remember someone for whom you are praying, commit them afresh into the care of God, ask for God's blessing to be upon them, ask that their needs be tended to. It takes only a few seconds, but it makes a healing, loving connection between you, them, and God. If you have run into them, stop for a moment and speak with them, check in, see how they are doing, discern in what if any ways you might be helpful to them, and listen to see what *you* might learn from *them* in this encounter. If something brings them to mind, take a moment and give them a quick call to let them know you were thinking of them. In such small acts of kindness, the healing powers of love are released, often in surprising ways.

Praying for Yourself on the Run

I have a friend who swears that when she is running late for an appointment and needs to quickly park her car, on the way to the appointment she prays fervently that God will find her a parking space—and it almost always works! She also gives God credit—in answer to her prayers—for helping her to find lost things. This is not what I have in mind when I suggest that you pray for yourself on the run.

The delightful little book called *The Practice of the Presence of God* is a collection of conversations with and letters from a seventeenth-century lay brother at a monastery in Paris. Brother Lawrence was at first a kitchen helper and then the cook for the monastery. He was a simple man who carried on a running conversation with God, not about parking spaces or lost keys, but about things that mattered both to himself and God. Which means he had to be mindful of what was going on. He kept an eye on himself. When something happened that challenged the values he wanted to live by, he would stop briefly and tell God, "I can't do this unless you help me."[15] And then he would get on with whatever he was doing.

For example, if you are in a situation that calls for patience and you notice that you are feeling impatient, stop for a moment and tell God: "This calls for patience, I want to be patient, and I'm not feeling patient at all. Help!" And then dive back into the situation that calls for patience. When compassion and gentleness are called for and you are feeling harsh or indifferent, take a moment and tell God: "I want to be compassionate and gentle here, but I'm just not. Help." And then look at what's going on again.

Any time in any situation or relationship, when you feel the need to express one or more of the fruit of the Spirit—love, joy, peace, patience, kindness, generosity, faithfulness, gentleness, self-control—and it seems beyond you, tell God how you want to be in that situation or relationship and ask for help. Get in the habit of carrying on such a conversation with God and you will discover what St. Paul did: "My [God's] grace is sufficient for you, for power is made perfect in weakness" (2 Corinthians 12:9). No shame in not being able to live the values you affirm. No pride in moments of seeming success. Just a humble trust that God's power is indeed made perfect in our weakness, and a willingness both to accept and follow God's help.

Of course, this kind of running conversation with God requires mindfulness. If you are losing patience, you need to notice that you are losing patience *before its gone*, and then take a moment for prayer. If kindness is getting lost in sudden anger, you need to notice the rising anger *before it takes over*, and then take a moment for prayer.

Brother Lawrence's running conversation with God was not only about being the way he wanted to be, but also about not being the way he didn't want to be. As St. Paul noted, "all have sinned and fall short of the glory of God" (Romans 3:23). No exceptions. As we move through the day, we all often fall short of the glory of God. When Brother Lawrence went through his day, as soon as he recognized a sinful thought, attitude, word, or action, he stopped, confessed to God on the spot, and said, "God, this is not the way I want to be, but it's the way I am, and so if I'm going to change, you'll have to change me." Then he got on with his life. He did not wallow in guilt. He recognized and owned his faults, confessed them, trusted in God's forgiveness, and in God's power to transform him. As St. John put it: "If we confess our sins, he who is faithful and just will forgive us our sins and cleanse us from all unrighteousness" (1 John 1:9).

To carry on this kind of mindful running conversation with God is to entrust oneself to God. It takes a certain humility and honesty; it leads to a growing sense of integrity and authenticity; it is the path to a more full humanity.

ORDINARY SANCTUARIES

Many years ago, I attended a conference on discipleship where I met a woman (I'll call her Anne) who told an amazing story. It seems she was a professor at Boston University and, like many people who live in large cities, she didn't own a car. She rode the bus between her home in the suburbs and the university campus. Each night she rode the same bus home, and it was an unnerving experience. The bus traveled through some tough streets in South Boston, and as people got on and off the bus there was a palpable tension in the air. The bus driver was always irritable. Many passengers looked angry, many looked fearful, many filled the space with loud, rude behavior, many cowered, trying not to be noticed. It was always with a sigh of relief that she reached the bus stop near her home and stepped off the bus onto familiar ground.

Occasionally Anne would find herself running late and she would miss her regular bus. She would then have to wait about twenty minutes to half an hour for the next bus. After this happened several times, she began to find herself hoping she would be late and miss her regular bus! There was something about the later bus. It felt safer. It felt warmer, somehow friendly. There wasn't the same tension, the same suspicious looks, the same sullenness that she had experienced on the earlier bus.

After several months of feeling uneasy each time she got on her regular bus, she found herself looking forward to riding the late bus. When she walked onto that late bus she felt an inexplicable peacefulness, not the nervousness she felt when climbing onto the early bus.

It was not a subtle difference. It was an unmistakable difference. She wondered if it had something to do with the driver. He greeted everyone who got on the bus with an expansive smile—even seemed to know the names of the regular riders. And Anne liked the way his voice followed people off the bus. "You have a good night now; God be with you now, you hear? You look for him now. He's out there."

One day Anne sat up at the front of the bus so she could talk with the driver as they drove through the dusky city streets. She told him how she felt on the early bus and how she felt on his bus—nervous and anxious on the early bus, relaxed and comfortable on his. She asked him what he thought accounted for that.

He smiled and said, "Well, I don't know much about that, but I can tell you that this bus is my sanctuary. When folks get onto my bus, I let them know I'm glad they're here, and as they walk back to get a seat, I watch them in the mirror and say a prayer for them. I don't know what they need, but God does, and so I just ask God to give them what they need—not what they want, but what they need. And I ask God's spirit to fill this bus and to be with everyone who rides the bus.

"And when folks get off, I send them on their way with a blessing. God's with them whether they know it or not so I just remind them of that. This bus . . . no stained glass, no organ, nothing like that, but this bus is my sanctuary and I'm just doing God's work by blessing people."

I found it to be a rather remarkable story. One bus was just a means of public transportation. The other was a sanctuary, a means of blessing. The driver of the first bus had a job. The driver of the second bus had a calling.

Do you work in an office? Make that office your sanctuary; make the people you work with, the clients you help, the vendors you use, the people who clean your office at night, make them all people to pray for, to serve, to bless. Work in a hospital or clinic? Make it your sanctuary, every colleague, every patient, every anxious or frightened patient visitor someone to pray for, to serve, to bless. Do you work in a retail store? Make it a sanctuary—every customer a parishioner, someone to pray for, to serve, to bless. Do you teach? Make your classroom a sanctuary. Do you take care of a family? Make your home a sanctuary.

No matter what you do, you do it somewhere and with someone, and you can turn that somewhere into a sanctuary by praying for the people who share that somewhere with you, by asking God to bless them, by being there for them when they need someone to be there for them, by helping them when help is needed. This is another way to make a healing, loving connection between you, others, and God, a way to open the places where you live and work and play to the energies of divine love.

THE PRAYER OF LOVING KINDNESS FOR CHRISTIANS

I can still remember my conversation some twenty years ago with a professor of world religions over a cup of green tea in the cafeteria of International Christian University in Japan. We were talking about prayer in the great religious traditions. He asked if I was familiar with the loving kindness prayer practiced by some schools of Buddhism. I said I wasn't, and he explained that it was a simple expression of a deep desire that all beings (no exceptions) be happy and at peace and experience loving kindness.

If you Google "prayer of loving kindness," you will find thousands of hits and many variations on the prayer. In its simplest form, as my friend explained, the prayer is a blessing:

May all beings be happy
May all beings be at peace
May all beings be filled with loving kindness[16]

He went on to say, that in a meditation on loving kindness, the one praying begins by asking the blessing on her- or himself:

May I be happy
May I be at peace
May I be filled with loving kindness

The one praying then moves on to pray the blessing for family and friends, for people they are close to: "May (name) be happy. . . ." Next one prays for those with whom they are angry or in conflict with: "May (name) be happy. . . ." After blessing these "enemies," one goes on to pray for groups of people: "May all Christians be happy. . . . May all Muslims be happy. . . . May all Israelis be happy. . . . May all Palestinians be happy." The trick is to ask this blessing for groups you identify with *and* groups you don't identify with, for all sides in a conflict. Finally, you end up with the universal blessing: "May all beings be happy. . . ."

In the days that followed this conversation, I mulled over this prayer. It seemed rather profound in its simplicity. If all people were happy, at peace, and filled with loving kindness, this world would be much different from the way it is now with all its unhappiness, violence, and hatefulness or indifference. Here was a prayer from another religious tradition that a Christian could easily pray, a prayer that could certainly be prayed in the name of Jesus.

I began to pray this blessing and began to feel that my own capacity for loving kindness was growing. I began to feel that this blessing did indeed connect with the energies of divine love. After some days, it occurred to me spontaneously to add a line to the blessing, and I began to pray:

> May you be happy
> May you be at peace
> May you be filled with loving kindness
> *May the Spirit of Jesus live in and through you*

With this addition, the prayer felt complete. The Spirit of Jesus is the Spirit of Love, the Spirit of Justice, the Spirit of Compassion and Mercy, the Spirit of Oneness with God and All of Creation. What a powerful blessing to seek for yourself and all other beings: that the Spirit of Jesus live *in and through* all of us.

For me, as a follower of Jesus, this blessing is grounded in God's vision for the world as expressed by the prophet Isaiah, what has been called the vision of the peaceable kingdom:

> The wolf shall live with the lamb,
>   the leopard shall lie down with the kid,
> the calf and the lion and the fatling together,
>   and a little child shall lead them.
> The cow and the bear shall graze,
>   their young shall lie down together;
>   and the lion shall eat straw like the ox.
> The nursing child shall play over the hole of the asp,
>   and the weaned child shall put its hand on the adder's den.
> *They will not hurt or destroy*
>   *on all my holy mountain;*
> *for the earth will be full of the knowledge of the LORD*
>   *as the waters cover the sea.* (Isaiah 11:6-9, emphasis added)

I recommend that you adopt this prayer of loving kindness for both your fixed time of prayer and as a powerful prayer on the run. At the beginning of your fixed time of prayer, before you get down to the specifics in your prayer list, spend a few minutes with this blessing prayer. First pray for yourself: "May I be happy. . . . May the Spirit of Jesus live in and through me." Then pray for people who are close to you, and move on to people you are acquainted with and like. Then pray for people you are acquainted with and don't like. Then pray for people you don't know but don't like. This prayer of blessing is one way to follow Jesus' direction to love our enemies and pray for those who would harm us (Matthew 5:44; Luke 6:27, 35). Also include "people groups," for example: "May all Americans be happy. . . ." "May all Iraqis be happy. . . ," and so forth. Pray for all sides in any conflict, even those you consider to be in the wrong. You don't have to be exhaustive; simply pray for whoever comes to mind in the moment, and then end by praying: "May all beings be happy. . . ."

Throughout the day, whenever you are personally feeling stressful, upset, frustrated, hurt, angry, selfish, unforgiving, just stop for a moment and pray: "May I be happy. . . ." When you see other people who seem stressful, upset, frustrated, hurt, angry, selfish, unforgiving, stop for a moment and pray: "May (name) be happy. . . ." Should someone hurt or offend you, bless them by praying: "May you be happy. . . ." When you cross the threshold at work, bless those who work with you: "May all in this office (or factory or store or school) be happy. . . ." It is not an onerous task—it takes about nine seconds; nine seconds that will transform your own attitudes and behavior and bring the energies of divine love into your workplace and relationships. When you enter a meeting, a restaurant, a bar and grill, a movie theater, a supermarket—wherever—bless everyone present with this simple but profound prayer:

May you all be happy
May you all be at peace
May you all be filled with loving kindness
May the Spirit of Jesus live in and through all of you

Nine seconds. Blessing others is a good habit, one completely in keeping with the words of the prophet Micah who insists that all God wants from us is that we do justice, love kindness, and walk humbly with our God (Micah 6:8).

LISTENING FOR THE VOICE OF GOD ON THE RUN

It may seem easier to listen for the voice of God in the relative silence and solitude of your fixed time of prayer than when on the run. There are less distractions and more focus when you are settled into your chair or onto your cushion. Away from the cell phone, computer, BlackBerry, and the constant and often conflicting demands of work and relationships that leave you feeling pushed and pulled in several directions at once, the single-minded intention to pray can open you to the word of God in the Bible and the word of God in the promptings of your conscience. Yes, it is easier to listen for the voice of God in times of silence and solitude, but it is not impossible to hear that voice when you are on the run.

As you go through the day and get involved in various events and interactions, it is always a good thing to stop every now and then and listen to what your conscience has to say about what's going on with you and with others. It is easy to dismiss the conscience with jokes about an angel sitting on one shoulder whispering in your ear while a devil sits on the other shoulder also whispering in your ear. Rather than give the conscience its due, all too often postmodern folks make decisions on the basis of either expediency or self-serving subjectivity. Christian tradition has, however, long insisted that:

> Fundamental revelations about God's intent for society and divine expectations for moral conduct are implanted in everyone's conscience, whether atheist or fervent faith-adherent. The "natural law" written into the warp and woof of the universe is available for all human beings to discern and follow.[17]

We are hard-wired by our creator to know right from wrong, and thus may take the promptings of our conscience in the midst of particular situations to be the still, small, persuasive voice of God encouraging us to do justice, to love kindness, to continue in the way of God. But it needs to be listened to.

Just this morning, I came back into the house after filling the bird feeders in the backyard. I was distracted, thinking about this chapter that I am writing right now! My wife, who was about to leave the house for an orchestra rehearsal, started talking to me about something important. I didn't hear a word she said. Suddenly I got the tone of seriousness in her voice and had to rewind, get free from the distraction of this book, and ask her to say it again.

As you go through the day, stop from time to time, and listen to what God might be saying to you in the murmurings of your conscience. Be intentional about it. Step back for a moment from conversations or activities and go within: do you feel good about what you're thinking, feeling, doing? Are you the way you want to be, doing the things you want to do the way you want to do them? Is what's going on good for me and good for others? Listen. And talk back to God about what you are hearing, seek wisdom and understanding, and the empowerment and wisdom of God's Spirit in the present moment when good choices need to be made and good actions taken.

TAKING THE WORD WITH YOU

In 1970 I decided to quit smoking—a decision I would not have had to make if I had been smart ten years earlier and not started! Over the ten years that I smoked, I stopped several times—at least I thought I had. Then one day a friend told me with uncomfortable bluntness that I had never quit smoking; I had simply deprived myself of the pleasure of a cigarette for a few days or weeks at a time. She was right.

When I finally made up my mind to really quit, she had a good suggestion: buy a pocket-sized New Testament and put it in my shirt pocket where I had been in the habit of carrying my cigarettes. Every time the urge to smoke came over me and I habitually reached for my shirt pocket, I should take out the New Testament, open it at random, and begin to read until my desire for a cigarette diminished and disappeared.

It was a very good idea. Not only did it distract me from thinking about smoking, I was filling my mind with the Word of God. I used to smoke two or more packs a day, so you can imagine how often I was pulling that New Testament from my pocket! I focused on reading the four Gospels, and before I knew it, Jesus' words were rolling around in my head (and heart) from morning to night, beginning to impact the way I was in the world. Time and again I would find myself suddenly praying, talking to God about what I had read and what it might mean for me in the concrete particularities of my life. I had begun to experience in real time what the psalmist meant when he or she wrote: "Your word is a lamp to my feet and a light to my path" (Psalm 119:105).

And so it should be for all who seek to follow Jesus in the way of God. I encourage you to go to your local bookstore or Amazon.com and purchase a small pocket-sized New Testament. Get one that also has the Psalms—most of them do. Put it in your shirt or suit coat pocket, or carry it in your briefcase or handbag. Take it out several times a day for just a few minutes. Read, and let the Word of God start rolling around in your head and heart, doing what the Word of God wants to do in and through you.

seven

MEDITATION / CONTEMPLATIVE PRAYER

My soul is satisfied as with a rich feast,
and my mouth praises you with joyful lips
when I think of you on my bed,
and meditate on you in the watches of the night;
for you have been my help,
and in the shadow of your wings I sing for joy.
—Psalm 63:5-7

During my senior year in the seminary, I had a crisis of faith, something not completely uncommon among seminary students. The closer one gets to graduation, ordination, and first call, the more one is faced with the utter seriousness of public ministry. At least, that was the case for me. My crisis of faith was serious enough that I considered leaving the seminary and not following what I had thought was a genuine call to ordained ministry.

My crisis of faith had to do with prayer. In a nutshell, it no longer made any sense to me. My prayer had turned dry as dust. I no longer felt connected to

God. When I prayed it seemed like I was either talking to myself or to a brick wall. My prayers seemed to float upwards like bubbles on the wind, bursting a few feet above the ground, leaving no trace, impacting nothing.

When I took the time to look hard at my prayers, to study their content, they seemed manipulative, nothing more than a laundry list of things I wanted God to do for me because I couldn't do them for myself. In a moment of spiritual honesty, I came to the conclusion that I was treating God like a cosmic butler. In prayer I would hand God my laundry list of needs and wants, expecting them to be taken care of. Of course, they never were (and shouldn't have been).

I found myself in a spiritual and moral quandary. In short, I could become a pastor and live a lie, or I could have some integrity, leave the seminary, and find some other helping profession in which to earn my living.

You see, pastors are always expected to pray: in Sunday worship, at the beginning and ending of meetings, beside hospital beds, at funerals and weddings, at graduation and confirmation parties, during pastoral counseling sessions and pastoral visits to shut-ins. Invite a pastor to dinner with a dozen other people and you know who will be asked to say grace before the meal. Day after day, over the telephone, in conversations before or after worship, in the aisles of the supermarket, people share their needs, their sorrows, their troubles and ask: "Pastor, would you please pray for me?" They expect—and have a right to expect—that their pastor will do just that.

You see my quandary: surrender my integrity, become a pastor, and go through the motions of prayer, or keep my integrity and find some other vocation to live out my calling to follow Jesus (something that can be done in most vocations). I struggled with this spiritual and moral dilemma for some time, and then I did what I always do when I have a problem—I looked for a book. I went to the library and looked up "prayer" in the card catalog.

There were surprisingly few books listed under "prayer." This was back in the early 1970s, and, unlike today, prayer was not part of the curriculum in Lutheran and other mainline Protestant seminaries. It was assumed that prayer was personal, not a subject for study, that we all knew how to do it. Most of us didn't.

Two of the books I found in the seminary library taught me what I needed to know about prayer to stay in school, finish the course, become ordained, and keep my feet on the path of prayer throughout thirty-three years as a Lutheran pastor and professor. The first one, called *Prayer,* was written in the 1930s by O. Hallesby, a Norwegian theologian and devotional writer. His book—written some eighty years ago—remains in print and is rightly considered a classic on prayer. It speaks as clearly in the early twenty-first century about the theology and practice of prayer as it did in the early twentieth century.

The second book that helped to solve my crisis of faith proved to be the most influential. *Contemplative Prayer* was written by Thomas Merton shortly before his tragic accidental death in 1968. Published in 1969, some six years before I found it in the seminary library, this little book introduced me to the long Christian tradition of contemplative prayer or Christian meditation. Over the years (thanks to finding this book), I have come to identify myself as a follower of Jesus who practices meditation, as a contemplative—one who lives a contemplative lifestyle.

THE DISTINCTION BETWEEN MEDITATION AND CONTEMPLATIVE PRAYER

The word meditation is often associated with Eastern religions; it's what Buddhists and Hindu yogis do. For this reason, until recently most Protestants (particularly conservative Protestants) have looked askance at meditation, seeing it as either a delusion or a danger, although meditation in various forms has a long history in the Roman Catholic and Eastern Orthodox traditions.

It is neither delusion nor danger. Meditation is an ancient Christian practice that draws one into that silence where God can be known in love. As Merton wrote, this prayer is a "wordless and total surrender of the heart [to God] in silence."[18] Or as God said through the psalmist: "Be still and know that I am God" (Psalm 46:10). Christian meditation and contemplative prayer are often called "the prayer of silence" or the "prayer of the heart," for it is in deep interior silence that we know, love, and rest in the God who is love (1 John 4:7-8).

The word meditation can be used in two primary ways. On the one hand it signifies a form of *mental prayer* in which the mind is deeply focused on a word or passage of the Bible, on a theological or doctrinal concept (for example, the doctrine of the Trinity, the full humanity and divinity of Christ, the omnipresence of God), or on religious virtues (such as the fruit of the Spirit: love, joy, peace, patience, kindness, generosity, faithfulness, gentleness, and self-control).

Meditation thought of in this way uses words. It involves focused, disciplined thinking, and so it is called discursive (using reason) meditation. Discursive meditation has been practiced since the very beginning when the earliest Christians "devoted themselves to the apostles' teaching" (Acts 2:42). It is that kind of meditation the psalmists refer to when they speak about meditating on the law, precepts, and ways of God (see, for example, Psalm 77:12; 119:15; 144:5).

On the other hand, however, non-discursive meditation uses no words; it is a *non-rational* resting in or communion with the God who transcends all concepts, all definitions, all images, and is only truly known in the silent mutuality of love. When used this way, the word meditation is interchangeable with "contemplation" or "contemplative prayer."

To say non-discursive meditation (contemplation) is non-rational is not to say that it is irrational. To be irrational is to be devoid of reason, meaning to be foolish, stupid, incoherent, or absurd. To be non-rational, however, is to go beyond reason, meaning to enter the realm of intuition. The dictionary describes intuition as "the act or faculty of knowing or sensing without the use of rational processes; *immediate cognition*."[19] Non-discursive meditation—contemplative prayer—leads to a knowing or sensing of God that does not come through thinking or the exercise of reason, but rather through an intuitive, immediate experience of God with and within us. It involves sitting in silence, and learning how to deal with the distracting thoughts and feelings that get in the way of our entering into an interior awareness of oneness with God. It involves surrendering ourselves to God in the movements of love.

I will first introduce discursive meditation, meditation that uses human reason to approach the Divine. I will then introduce non-discursive meditation or contemplative prayer. Although I will give some suggestions for beginning in Christian contemplative prayer, in a primer on prayer such as this, it is impossible to explore the subject to the length and depth it deserves. At the back of this book, I have listed suggestions for further reading that will help you make that exploration should you feel called to walk a contemplative path.

DISCURSIVE MEDITATION

As mentioned above, discursive meditation uses words and encourages deep and careful reflection on the meaning of those words. It requires directed awareness and deep concentration. The focus of your meditation can be anything that opens you both to an awareness of God and an awareness of yourself in relationship to God. Discursive meditation helps to provide the deep content upon which the life of faith is built.

There are many suitable objects of meditation:

- The idea of God
- A passage from scripture
- A passage from a spiritual book
- A hymn lyric
- Poetry
- The mysteries of faith
- The creation
- An object such as a candle, a cross or crucifix, bread and wine, water.

Choose something with which you have an affinity. My wife Bobbi is a church musician, and meditation on hymn lyrics takes her into that deep place where both her awareness of God and awareness of her relationship with God are strengthened. Once Bobbi and I spent a weekend at a hermitage. While I spent the time in the silence of contemplative prayer in my hermitage, she spent the weekend singing hymns and reflecting on their deep meaning in hers.

A friend from one of my meditation groups meditates using a candle— a symbol of Jesus as the light of the world (John 8:12, 9:5), and a symbol of Jesus' followers as the light of the world (Matthew 5:14). The teachings of Jesus in the Gospels are a rich source of meditation for people with a love of reading. Religious icons are also a rich source of meditation for people who are visually oriented.[20]

Objects suitable for meditation, for deep thought and introspection, are numerous. Pick one that works for you. Stay with it for as long as it takes to exhaust (at least for the moment) its meaning, or until some other compelling reason to change your meditation focus arises. You can return to anything you have previously meditated on at any time should it seem right to you.

To begin the process of discursive meditation, go to your fixed place of prayer, and sit in your chair or settle onto your cushion. Ask the Holy Spirit to grant you wisdom and guide your meditation. Get centered by becoming aware of your breathing. For a few moments, simply focus your awareness on the rise and fall of your abdomen or chest, or on the sensation of your breath entering and leaving your nostrils. As you breathe, remember that breath is both life and gift from the One who made you (Genesis 2:7; Psalm 33:6; 104:29).

When you feel centered, begin to direct your attention on the focus of your meditation:

- If the focus of your meditation is a passage from the Bible, some other book, or perhaps a hymn lyric or poem, slowly read the words whose meaning you are going to focus on. Do it several times until the words begin settling into your mind and heart.

Spend time reflecting on each word by itself and in combination with the other words that surround it.

- Ask yourself what it means in general terms.
- Ask yourself what it means specifically for you in your present circumstances.
- Ask yourself what it means for you as a member of a community of faith.
- Ask yourself if any changes in attitude or behavior are suggested by the text.

When you come to the end of your meditation, take out your journal and record your reflections.

- If the focus of your meditation is an idea (for example, the notion of God, the idea of love or forgiveness or reconciliation, the mercy of God, or the death of Jesus), repeat the word or phrase that expresses your meditation object in sync with your breath until it settles into your heart and mind. If you have chosen to meditate on love, each time you inhale, gently repeat the word "love" in your mind; as you exhale, repeat the word again. If you have chosen to meditate on "the mercy of God," repeat the phrase in the silence of your mind each time you inhale, and again each time you exhale. Once you have a taste for the word or phrase, begin to reflect deeply on all aspects of its meaning.
- What does it mean in general terms?
- What does it mean specifically for you in the context of your present life and relationships?
- What does it mean for your community of faith?
- Does your meditation suggest any changes in attitude or behavior?

When you have come to the end of your meditation, open your journal and record your reflections and conclusions.

• If the focus of your meditation is a physical item, for example, a candle, cross, or water, place it in front of you. Begin by concentrating on your breathing, as described above, until you feel settled and at peace. Then direct your attention deeply on your meditation object. Look at it carefully; pick it up, notice whatever details there are.

- • Explore its metaphorical or symbolic meaning in general terms.
- • Reflect on the meaning of the object for your own faith and relationship with God within the concrete realities of your life.
- • Explore the meaning of the object for your community of faith.
- • Reflect on any changes in attitude or behavior suggested by your meditation.

Again, before leaving your place of prayer, record your reflections and conclusions in your journal.

I would suggest that you practice discursive meditation once a week for twenty to thirty minutes. In the week between meditation sessions, read through your previous journal entries in order to keep the insights and questions of your last meditation in front of you. It is always a good idea to discuss your insights and questions with a pastor or spiritual friend. Remember, the spiritual journey is not a heroic solitary journey; it is a journey in company with fellow travelers on the way of God. It only makes sense to learn from each other, correct each other, encourage each other along the way.

NON-DISCURSIVE MEDITATION / CONTEMPLATIVE PRAYER

In what follows, I will be using the words meditation and contemplative prayer interchangeably to speak of that prayer that seeks to still the mind and usher you into that silence where God dwells in the immensity and immediacy of love. The purpose of such prayer is to commune with God without words, concepts, or images. It is to go beyond all words and thought into an immediate awareness of God present to you and within you in the mystery of divine love.

Unfortunately, there is much that stands in the way of such an immediate awareness of God. Our attention is all too easily distracted by this, that and the next thing. Our heads are constantly filled with noise—thoughts, feelings, imaginings. God can *only* be experienced in the present moment, and we spend so little time in the present moment that it is not unusual for us to miss the Divine among and within us.

When I was in seminary, I took a class called, "Introduction to Pastoral Care," taught by a very wise and gentle man by the name of Bill Smith. In one class, when we were talking about Gestalt therapy, Bill noted that most of us spend 90 percent or more of our time either rehashing the past or rehearsing the future and only 10 percent or less of our time actually in the present moment. Which is to say that we spend 90 percent or more of our time living in an illusion, and only ten percent or less of our time in reality. The present moment is real, it's what's happening, it's where God is present, and we miss most of it because we spend so much time living in the past or the future.

Thanks to the process of "selective memory," the past that we spend so much time rehashing is not the past that really was. The remembered good times, the glories and successes, pleasures and perks of the past are not what really happened; nor are the remembered hurts, offenses, slights, mistakes and failures, liabilities and losses. Memory embellishes and distorts. The "remembered" past is largely illusion, but an illusion with tremendous power to control our thoughts and feelings, keeping them tied to the past. God cannot be experienced in the past.

Nor can God be experienced in the future. As we all know from our own experience, the future, when it finally arrives and becomes the present moment, is never how we imagined it would be. No matter how much we rehearse the future, it will be different than what we either feared or hoped for. And yet that illusory prospect has tremendous power to control our thoughts and feelings, keeping them tied to a dim and ever receding vista of threat or promise.

My friend and teacher, Bill, suggested that we reverse the numbers, that we spend about ten percent of the time learning what can be learned from the past and making reasonable preparations for the future, and ninety percent of our time living in the present moment, aware of and engaged with what is actually happening. I have spent the last thirty-six years of my life trying to do just that. Meditation has been for me the path out of the past and future and into the present moment.

Of course, living in the present moment will most often mean noticing, thinking about, and responding to what has just happened. It means that you are not quite in the present moment—close but not quite in. You see, when you are thinking about something you are at least one step back from the experience (or one step ahead of the experience) and so the immediacy of the experience is lost, although it is still close enough to be felt. Mentally, emotionally, and spiritually, living in the present moment in this sense is far healthier and much more authentic than living in the past and/or the future, even if it is not really *being* in the present moment.

It is not easy to really be in the present moment. We think too much. Have you ever been lost in an experience, simply aware of what's happening without thinking about it? Time seems to stop. Lost in the beauty of a sunset or in the face of a beloved, not thinking, just present to what is, have you ever had a feeling of oneness and communion that transcends the narrow boundaries of your ego? Such experiences—which most of us have had—are experiences of being in the present moment. Meditation leads to this experience of immediacy, the experience of being *in* the present moment when what's happening is God.

I often tell my students that meditation is "the art of letting go"— letting go of the thoughts, feelings, and imaginings that fill our minds and hearts and turn our attention away from what's really going on in the here and now. Meditation is, to use an expression learned from a Japanese friend, a way to "tame the monkey mind" that runs to and fro, flitting from this to that, never settling down into silence.

The regular practice of meditation will:

- Help you develop a deep interior silence within which you can more readily focus your attention and rest in a simple awareness of what is.
- Help you consistently to live in the present moment in the sense of being only a step or two, rather than miles and miles, away from what is happening in the present moment.
- Bring you from time to time fully into the present moment and the immediate experience of God, the experience of communion and union with the One in whom "we live and move and have our being."

It should be noted that what we do in meditation does not command God's presence, it opens us to God's presence. It clears away the clutter of our minds and hearts so that we may see what is already there—God. Meditation is not a work of righteousness; it is an opening to grace.

In the Gospel of Matthew, Jesus declared:

The eye is the lamp of the body. So, if your eye is healthy, your whole body will be full of light; but if your eye is unhealthy, your whole body will be full of darkness. If then the light in you is darkness, how great is the darkness! (Matthew 6:22-23)

Contemplative prayer is a healing of that eye, a process of learning to see.

How can you know if contemplative prayer is for you?

I have taught contemplative prayer for many years, both one-on-one and in small meditation groups. In all those years, I never asked anyone if they wanted to learn meditation. I would let people know that I practiced contemplative prayer, and in answer to questions would talk about it, but I would not issue an invitation to learn. In my experience, when it comes to meditation, the old saying is true: "When the student is ready, the teacher appears." If the student is not ready, a hundred teachers cannot teach him. If the student is ready, she will find a teacher—be it a book or a person.

I am not suggesting that mediation is some esoteric practice that is not meant for everyone but only for the spiritually elite. Not at all. To my mind, the contemplative experience is open to all. I am suggesting, however, that it helps if the student is ready, if they have reached a point in their spiritual journey where they feel deeply called into the silence beyond words where the divine mystery dwells and beckons us through the persuasive power of love.

To begin the practice of meditation—this "work of love"—when you are not ready will most likely lead to your abandoning it at some point and not returning to it. To begin when your spiritual history has prepared you for it, will most likely lead you to integrate meditation into the warp and woof of your life, a life that can then be called contemplative.

So how do you know when you're ready? When someone comes to me and asks me to teach them meditation, I usually pour us both a cup of coffee and ask them two questions. First, I have them read the following verses from the Psalms, the prayer book of the Bible:

> As a deer longs for flowing streams,
>   so my soul longs for you, O God.
> My soul thirsts for God,
>   for the living God.
> When shall I come and behold
>   the face of God? (Psalm 42:1-2)
>
> O God, you are my God, I seek you,
>   my soul thirsts for you;

my flesh faints for you,
    as in a dry and weary land where there is no water. (Psalm 63:1)

Be still, and know that I am God. (Psalm 46:10)

For God alone my soul waits in silence;
    from him comes my salvation. . . .
For God alone my soul waits in silence,
    for my hope is from him. (Psalm 62:1, 5)

Then I ask them simply to tell me what the texts mean to them; in what ways, if any, do they resonate with their own experience. And so let me ask you: do these texts resonate with your experience? Do they reflect your longing for a deeper experience of God? Do they express your love for God? Do they evoke a desire for interior silence within which love becomes the medium of communion and union with God?

Put the book down for a moment and answer these questions in your journal.

If you feel a growing desire for meditation, a growing desire for more intimacy with God, a growing need to express the inexpressible love for God that seems to flow through you, then you are likely ready to begin the practice of meditation. If silence is beginning to feel not like the absence of God but like the presence of God, then you are most likely ready to begin this work of love.

Next I ask people who want to learn meditation to tell me about their prayer life. How long have you been disciplined about the practice of prayer? What do you pray about? Do you pray more about yourself or others? How often do you pray? Do you carry on a running conversation with God throughout the day? Do you practice discursive meditation on the Bible?

Then I ask them to tell me about the feeling tone of their prayer. Is it easy or hard to pray? If hard now, was it easier before? If easy now, does your time of prayer give you feelings of joy and peace? Does verbal prayer turn you on or is it starting to turn you off? Does your prayer feel dry as dust or as sweet as a glass of cold, fresh spring water? Do you feel like you are only going through the motions out of religious obligation or duty, or do you have an inner compulsion to pray?

Without reading on, put the book down for a moment and answer these questions in your journal.

If you feel a strong compulsion to verbal prayer and experience great joy and peace in prayer, along with a growing intimacy with and connection to God, then you are likely ready to add contemplative prayer to your practice. A strong and vibrant prayer life in fixed times and throughout the day is a good sign that you have a good foundation for contemplative practice.

However, although it may seem surprising, if you're just hanging in there with verbal prayer and discursive meditation in spite of the fact that you have begun to feel more and more unable to pray effectively, then that too might well be a sign that you are ready for contemplative prayer. When words become stale and seem ineffective, it may be a call to communion with God in loving, trusting silence. If you have a desire for greater intimacy with God and your thirst for God is not quenched in the work of discursive prayer, then this work of love may be calling you. You may be ready to enter that empty but full silence where love is an embrace of the Divine, not a word.

Take a moment to reflect in your journal as to whether or not you presently feel called to contemplative prayer.

Getting started in contemplative prayer

As you have probably noticed, it is difficult to speak with precision about the experience of contemplative prayer. People who follow a meditative path are often reduced to the language of poetry—

metaphor, simile, symbol, image, paradox—in the struggle to express that which finally cannot be truly expressed, but can only be experienced. All of which is to say that what matters is practice, practice, practice. Meditate, and in the grace of God, you will come more and more to experience for yourself that which can be known in the heart, but cannot be very well expressed by the mind.

Practice at least once and preferably twice a day. In the beginning, practice a minimum of twenty minutes a time. Forty minutes is best, but build up to it lest the strenuousness drive you away from this practice. When I meditate at home, it is usually for thirty or forty minutes. When I am on retreat, I mediate for fifty minutes, stand and stretch for ten minutes, then settle onto my cushion for another fifty minutes of meditation, and so pass the day. I have a watch with a countdown timer that keeps the time for me when I am time-constrained. When time is not of the essence, my inner clock knows how long I have been on my cushion and when it's time to rise from prayer and return to the activities that fill my days.

In the beginning, practice at the same time(s) each day in order to establish a contemplative rhythm in your daily life. In time you will find yourself able to meditate in a crowded airport waiting for your flight, but in the beginning, set times of practice will help you develop the interior silence that makes meditating in the noise and busyness of an airport (or anywhere else) possible.

Go to your prayer room, nook, corner, or alcove in your home. Enter your prayer space reverently, perhaps with a small bow of the head, your hands folded or palms together over your chest. Settle into your chair or onto your cushion. You may want to light a candle and/or ring a bell to signal the beginning of your mediation. When the meditation is over, extinguish the candle and/or ring the bell again. When you arise from meditation to return to the business and busyness of the day, once again reverence your prayer space with a brief bow or by making the sign of the cross. Such simple rituals are bodily reminders and affirmations of the sacred time, space, and action of contemplative prayer.

The process of contemplative prayer

It should be said that there is no one way of Christian meditation. There are a variety of ways to meditate, all of them sharing the goal of opening the meditator to the reality of divine grace and the ubiquity of God's loving presence. What I am sharing with you here is a method of practice that has worked well for me and others, and that will set your feet on the path to contemplative prayer. At the back of the book, I have suggested several books that might encourage you and help you continue on the path.

As the first step on the path to contemplative prayer, I would like to you to choose a word that expresses for you your longing for God, your love for God, your trust in God, a word that signifies for you the deep yearning of faith for communion and union with the author of faith. Choose a word that, in the words of the anonymous author of the fourteenth century spiritual classic, *The Cloud of Unknowing*, expresses your "naked intention" to "lift your heart to God with humble love."[21]

You will use this word to wean you gently from the many thoughts, emotions, and feelings (both physical and mental) that will distract you from this "work of love." To follow the advice of the author of *The Cloud of Unknowing*, choose a short word of one or maybe two syllables.[22] Over the years, I have mostly used the name "Jesus," as that is a name into which I can place all my faith, love, and trust. It is a word that holds my intention to lift my heart to God. It is a single word that speaks volumes for me without my having to think or say another word. That's what you want your word to do.

You might choose the word *God*, or perhaps *Yahweh*, the Hebrew name of God revealed to Moses in Exodus 3. You might simply choose the word *love* or *peace* or *mercy*. John Main, who did much to make the practice of Christian meditation accessible to ordinary Christians, recommends the Aramaic word *maranatha*, which can be translated as "come, Lord."[23] Any word into which you can place your faith, love and trust in God, and that expresses your intention to enter into the silence where God is known in love, will do.

Take a moment now to choose a word that works for you. Repeat it to yourself, both out loud and silently. Can you place your faith, love, and trust in God into the word so that it expresses your desire for God without your having to think or say another word? Take your time. If a word feels right, choose it, remembering that after praying with it for a few days, you can choose another if it no longer feels right.

When you meditate, whether you are in a chair or on a cushion, keep your back straight. It is easier to maintain your position—you don't want to move while meditating—and a slumped back can impede the flow of blood through your body, leading to grogginess if not sleepiness. If you are using a chair, choose a hard chair with a straight back. Keep your feet flat on the floor, hands folded or placed palms up in your lap, eyes closed, head slightly bent forward.

Say a brief prayer, asking God's blessing on the work you are about to do. Then begin to mentally repeat your word—once with each inhalation and once with each exhalation. Do not try to control your breathing; breathe normally, and with each in-breath, repeat your word, with each out-breath, repeat your word.

If your mind wanders—and it will, especially in the beginning—gently and without scolding yourself, go back to repeating your word in sync with your breathing. Don't *think* about your word or anything else. Let your meditation be an expression of your love for God, and simply rest beyond thought in the presence of God and in the love and blessing of God.

Thoughts, feelings, imaginings will come; simply note their presence and let them go, returning to the interior repetition of your word. A thought is not a distraction unless it becomes a *chain* of thought. If you think of a report you need to complete at work, and then think of the meeting where you will present the report, and then think of the people who will be at the meeting, and then feel anxiety over whether the report will be well received, and then start worrying about job security, and then wonder what you would tell your spouse if you failed to get a promotion or even lost your job, and then remembered that you are meeting your spouse for lunch, and then wonder what restaurant to go to, and then remember that little pasta place over on Seventh Avenue. . . . That's a chain of thought, and a major distraction from this "work of love" you are doing. It will happen. As soon as you notice that you have left your word and climbed on this rushing train of thought, simply go back to your word and continue repeating it as you breathe in and as you breathe out. In time, your chains of thought will grow shorter as you recognize them more quickly, and eventually, when thoughts, feelings, and imaginings arise, you will notice them right away, let them go, and continue with your word in rhythm with your breathing. Remember, meditation is the art of letting go. A thought arises, let it go. A feeling arises, let it go. Your imagination goes to work, let it go.

In the beginning, you will find yourself repeating your word, losing it to a chain of thought, and dealing with distractions for the whole of your meditation. You may feel frustrated; don't be. It's natural. Do not bring any expectations of what your experience should be with you into meditation other than the expectation to sit as long as you have chosen to sit. If you have a pleasurable feeling or thought while you meditate, don't get attached to it; notice it and let it go. If you have an unpleasant feeling or thought during your meditation, don't get attached to it; notice it and let it go. After the meditation is over, you can reflect back on the experience, and if there were any distracting thoughts, feelings or imaginings that seem worth pursuing, pursue them, perhaps in your journal.

In time, you will find distractions diminishing both in number and in the power to coalesce into a chain of thought. As interior distractions diminish, interior silence deepens, that silence in which you begin to experience yourself more and more deeply in communion and union with God in the mystery of divine love. From time to time, as the silence deepens, you may find yourself spontaneously letting go of your word and simply resting beyond all words, all concepts, all images in oneness with the Triune God, an experience of the mystery

Jesus declared when he told his followers: "On that day you will know that I am in my Father, and you in me, and I in you" (John 14:20).

At first, such moments of deep silence will be short, measured in seconds. In time they will grow longer. When distractions pull you out of this deep silence, gently return to the repetition of your word in rhythm with your breathing. Don't become attached to the experience of this mystery; it can't be forced. Just stay with your word and let it lead you back into silence, and each time you return from the silence, return to your word.

Eventually, if you are faithful to your practice, most of your meditation will be spent in this deep interior silence. No one can say how long that will take for any given person; it may be a matter of months or a matter of years. It doesn't matter. What matters is simply presenting yourself to God and resting in the mutuality of love.

As you continue to practice meditation, you will find that the interior silence within which God is known in love that you experience in meditation begins to carry over into the events and interactions of your day. The ability—developed in the practice of meditation—to let go of distractions and be in each moment with sharply focused concentration can channel awareness of the Divine into consciousness even when you are busy about other things. When this happens, take it as a sign that you are developing a contemplative lifestyle, one in which the experience of communion and union with the Transcendent can arise at any time and in any place.

CONCLUDING THOUGHTS ON CONTEMPLATIVE PRAYER

Words are inadequate to communicate profound experiences to those who have not had those experiences. Words can only hint at the length and breadth and depth of the encounter with the Triune God in the seeming emptiness of interior silence; they cannot make it happen; they cannot contain it. Words may offer something like a map of the territory, but they are not the territory. Armchair travelers pouring over their maps will never know the terrain or experience its wonder and beauty unless they put the map away, step out into the world, and start walking through it. As an old Russian proverb put it: "There is no path; we make the path by walking." This book is not a path; you make the path by your spiritual practice. As Thomas Merton noted: "The spiritual life is first of all a *life*. It is not merely something to be known and studied, it is to be lived."[24]

Contemplative prayer is part of a complete Christian life of faith. It doesn't replace other kinds of prayer and discursive meditation; it complements them and deepens them. The Christian life of faith is indeed *a life*, and it is a life measured by growth in love. Contemplation serves such growth; if it does not, it is false, having nothing to do with God. "For God so loved the world" he sent Jesus into the world for love, and God continues to send God's people into the world for love. Prayer that isolates you from the world, prayer that causes you to stand apart and judge and condemn the world has nothing to do with the contemplative experience of communion and union with the God who is love in deep interior silence.

It is not a good idea to measure your progress in living a spiritual life; it all too often leads to spiritual pride and thus distancing from God. If there is, however, one measure of the spiritual life that leads more to humility than pride, it is the measure of love. Growth in love is a reliable sign that it is God—and not our egos—with whom we commune in the practices of the spiritual life.

It is, therefore, a good idea to keep in conversation with a spiritual director or spiritual friend about your experiences with contemplative prayer. A wise guide or friend can keep you from stumbling, keep you honest, support and encourage you.

{afterword}

PRAYER—
THIS IS WHO I AM;
THIS IS WHAT I DO

Then Jesus told them a parable
about their need to pray always
and not to lose heart.
—Luke 18:1

Years ago there was a TV series that opened each week with the same scene. A young policeman is running down the street, chasing a fleeing criminal. The criminal runs into a parking garage and the policeman follows. The criminal fires at him, shattering the window in a parked car. The policeman rolls over the hood of the car, pulls his gun, and fires back. And just before the credits start to roll across the screen, the voice of the hero can be heard saying: "I'm a cop; that's who I am, that's what I do."

That sense of single-mindedness, focus, and devotion to calling impressed me then, and still does. When what you do becomes who you are, there is an authenticity and integrity to your calling. I hope that after having worked your way through this book, you have come to the place where you can say: "I'm a prayer; that's who I am, that's what I do."

When I was living and working in Japan, I was visited by a friend from back home (we'll call him George). He had never been to Japan before and so we did all the touristy things that first time visitors to a place do. We visited all the sights that ought to be seen, ate all the foods that ought to be eaten, went to the public bath that ought to be experienced, packed ourselves into the crowded trains and subways that ought to be ridden. We had a great time. After having lived there for many years, it was fun to see Japan again through the eyes of someone who had never been there before.

One day we went to the city of Kamakura to see the Great Buddha (*Daibutsu* in Japanese), a towering and impressive outdoor statue of the Buddha. After taking the obligatory pictures of the Buddha, we went up into the hills behind the Buddha on a path that would eventually take us to a small and unique Shinto shrine nestled in the mountains. As we walked through the beauty of a late spring day, George kept asking questions. Where were we going? How long would it take to get there? What was the shrine like? What would we do when we got there? How would we get back from the shrine? Where were we going for lunch? What would we eat?

Suddenly I stopped walking; George continued for another fifteen to twenty feet before he noticed I was no longer beside him. He turned around and asked: "What are you doing?"

"Good question," I responded. "What are we doing, George?"

He thought for a moment and then said, "Hiking in the mountains."

"Absolutely correct," I said. "So let's do that; let's hike. When we get to the shrine, you will know how long it took to get there, what it's like, and what we are going to do there. When we leave, you will know the path we are taking back. When we get to the restaurant, you will know where we are going to eat, and when you get your food, you will know what you are going to eat. Right now, let's be in this moment; let's hike."

"OK," he said. "Makes sense."

"Remember, George," I said as we resumed walking. "Anyone can *take* a hike; the point is to *be* a hiker."

Anyone can throw out a quick prayer in a moment of crisis or need or obligation, and then go back to the distractions of living in the past or the future with little, if any, reference to God. The point is to *be* a prayer, to be someone for whom ongoing communion with God is as natural as breathing.

My wife Bobbi is a musician. Music is not something she *does*; it is who she *is*. She didn't become the music overnight. Her innate capacity for music was nourished and cultivated through years of practice. So it is with prayer. Our innate capacity for relationship, for communion with the God in whose image we have been created, needs to be nourished through practice until it can be said of us, "You are the prayer."

And if we have done our practice well, if we have become a prayer, then perhaps it will also be said of us, "You are love,"—for that's what the Christian life of faith is all about.

REFLECTION, JOURNALING, AND IDEAS FOR PRACTICE

CHAPTER 1

Questions for Reflection
- In what ways is it true that prayer is the heart of the life of faith?
- Do you agree that we have a "*built-in desire* to be close to the God in whose image we were all created"? Why or why not?
- How do you understand the paradox that we are "being transformed" by the Spirit into the likeness of Christ while at the same time we must "work out" our own salvation? How would you apply this paradox to the practice of prayer?

Journaling Suggestions
- Write in your journal about the place of prayer in your life right now as you begin this book. Describe how, when, and for what you pray. Is prayer a joy or a job for you? Why? Are you satisfied with your present prayer life? Why or why not? What questions do you have about prayer that you hope this book will answer?
- Write a brief meditation on your desire for God.
- Do you sometimes fear that taking God more seriously might take you places you don't want to go? Explain.

Ideas for Pactice
- Practice using the awareness of your breath to get centered. Sit comfortably with your back straight, eyes closed, hands in your lap.

Breathe through your nose and focus your attention on your nostrils. Don't try to control your breath; just feel it coming in and going out. If you get distracted and your attention wanders, just bring it gently back to your breath. Remember that breath is a gift of God, the gift of life itself (Genesis 2:7; Psalm 104:29-30).

- Each time you take time to pray, begin by spending a few minutes following your breath. It will relax you and help you to settle into prayer with a deep sense of peace.
- Throughout the day, if you feel tense or stressed, take a few moments to practice awareness of your breath. It will relieve the tension or stress and help you to deal more calmly with whatever is at hand.
- On Sunday as you wait for worship to begin, practice awareness of the breath. It will prepare you for worship and open you to the encounter with God in word and sacrament.

CHAPTER 2

Questions for Reflection

- In what ways does the concept of "beginner's mind" make sense or not make sense to you?
- Do you find the concept of beginner's mind and the unlearning necessary to develop it to be threatening or exciting? Explain.
- Why is it important to say that "all our truths are small t truths"?

Journaling Suggestions

- Describe your mind. Is it beginner's mind? Explain.
- Write about the obstacles you might face in achieving and/or keeping beginner's mind.
- As part of the unlearning process, make a list of "What is?" questions that you want to ask.

Ideas for Practice

- Choose one of the "What is?" questions from the list in your journal. Begin to read through the Gospels, making a note of anything that might seem to be part of the answer to the question. If your reading raises questions, jot them down. If you get a flash of insight, make a note of it. If you are excited about what you find, or find yourself resisting what you find, make a note. If changes in thought, attitude, or behavior are suggested by what you discover, write them down too.

- As you go through the day, be mindful of times when you seem to be close-minded, conventional in your thinking, controlled by habit, biased, prejudiced, or opinionated. When you notice such things, be intentional about practicing beginner's mind. Record and reflect on your experience in your journal.

CHAPTER 3

Questions for Reflection

- Why will praying "in the name of Jesus" not win you the lottery?
- Do you find WWJD (What would Jesus do?) helpful as a guide for deciding what to pray about? Explain.
- What does it mean to say that "prayer . . . has to do with human transformation," that it "involves learning to have within us 'the same mind that was in Christ Jesus'"?

Journaling Suggestions

- Make a list in your journal of things/people/situations that you have recently prayed about. Circle those that seem most to be prayers "in the name of Jesus."
- Describe in your journal a situation or relationship in which you have a conflict or are unsure about how to proceed. Then write out your answer to the question: "What would Jesus do?"
- Write about times when your prayer seemed to be unanswered. In what ways might your prayer have been answered in ways other than you had hoped for?

Ideas for Practice

- If you didn't follow the suggestions in this chapter for starting a prayer list while you were reading, take the time to do it now. You will find the instructions on pages 35, 36, 37, 39.
- You cannot answer the question "What would Jesus do?" if you don't have a good idea of what Jesus would do. Read through the Gospels and make a list of Jesus' values. Note instances of how his actions and relationships reflected those values.
- As you go through the day, try using WWJD as a benchmark in moral decision making and as a guide to how you are in your relationships.
- Don't let WWJD become a rigid, legalistic way of approaching life. In every situation and relationship, practice beginner's mind; use

WWJD with beginner's mind. Keep an open mind—fresh, curious, and enthusiastic, with a deep sense of possibilities unfolding. The general answer to WWJD is love. Be open to the limitless possibilities of love when wondering what Jesus would do.

CHAPTER 4

Questions for Reflection

- What is the place of the Lord's prayer in your personal life of faith? In the life of your community of faith?
- What does it mean to say: "We never pray this prayer (or any prayer) alone"?
- What does the Lord's prayer tell us about how to pray and what to pray for?

Journaling Suggestions

- Write about the feelings that the expression "Our Father" in the Lord's Prayer evoke in you.
- Reflect in your journal on the idea that when we pray we are both asking God to act in answer to our prayer and expressing our own willingness to act in answer to our prayer. Give some examples of how this might be true.
- Paul said we should "owe no one anything, except to love one another" (Romans 13:8). In your journal, reflect on your circle of family, friends, co-workers, and acquaintances. Make a list of the ways in which Paul's advice is followed or not followed in these relationships. Does forgiveness need to be either asked for or given? What will you do?

Ideas for Practice

- If you didn't follow the suggestions in this chapter for adding to your prayer list from the petitions in the Lord's Prayer while you were reading, take the time to do it now. You will find the instructions on pages 46, 48, 50.
- Develop the practice of bookending each day with a slow, meditative reciting of the Lord's Prayer. Let it be the last thing you do before sleeping and the first thing you do upon awakening.
- Develop the practice of thanking God for "brother this" and "sister that" as you walk through the day. Be mindful of what and who are

around you. Thank you God for sister flower. Thank you God for Brother John. Record and reflect on the practice in your journal.

CHAPTER 5

Questions for Reflection

- Do you like the way this book expands the concept of prayer from simply talking to God to all the ways in which we communicate? Explain.
- What are some of the obstacles you might face in trying to set aside a fixed time and place for prayer? How might those obstacles be overcome?
- What differences are there between seeing prayer as something you do from time to time and seeing prayer as a way of life?

Journaling Suggestions

- Go back and read the prayer of Thomas Merton on page 63. Reflect in your journal on how, if at all, Merton's prayer resonates with your own experience.
- Reflect on whether your life feels like it has healthy rhythms or whether it feels fragmented—pushed and pulled in hundreds of directions by obligations and/or the needs of other people. Reflect on the ways in which a fixed time and place of prayer may add to your sense of healthy rhythms.
- Write a brief meditation on what it means to you to be "involved in humankind."

Ideas for Practice

- If you have not already done so, create a sacred space for prayer in your home.
- Review the practice of spiritual journaling on pages 73-75. Set a time for journaling and keep it faithfully.
- Memorize the Prayer of St. Francis on page 62. As you go through the day, if any of the petitions of that prayer seem appropriate to the situation you're in, pray them.

CHAPTER 6

Questions for Reflection

- Why is it as important to pray "on the run" as it is to have fixed times and places for prayer?
- In what ways does it (or doesn't it) make sense to think of your work space as a "sanctuary"?
- Are you comfortable with using prayers from other religious traditions—such as the loving kindness prayer—in Christian devotion and practice? Why or why not?

Journaling Suggestions

- Reflect in your journal on the ways in which you presently pray on the run. Are there any suggestions in this book for praying on the run that you plan on trying? How would you work them into your daily routine?
- Meditate on the fruit of the Spirit—love, joy, peace, patience, kindness, generosity, faithfulness, gentleness, self-control. Which, if any, of these fruits need a bit more cultivation? Would mindfulness of what's going on with you throughout the day coupled with prayer on the run for the Spirit's power help in the cultivation? Why or why not?
- Meditate on the spiritual practice of intentionally blessing others. How does (or might) the practice of blessing others impact your relationships?

Ideas for Practice

- Develop the practice of checking in with yourself from time to time throughout the day. How do you feel about yourself and the situation you are in? Do you feel good, bad, or indifferent about what you are doing? Do you hear the voice of God in the promptings of your conscience, leading you in one direction or another? Is there anything that needs to be prayed about right now?
- Memorize the loving kindness prayer on page 86, and use it both in times of fixed prayer and throughout the day to surround people with the blessings of God's love.
- Buy a pocket sized New Testament with Psalms and never leave home without it. Now and again throughout the day, take the time to read a few verses, and ask yourself what God might be saying to you in what you read in the context in which you read it.

CHAPTER 7

Questions for Reflection

- Are you comfortable with silence or somewhat intimidated or threatened by it? Explain.
- Discursive meditation gives you the "deep content" needed to build a life of faith. Non-discursive meditation gives you a "deep experience" of the God faith points to. Which kind of meditation do you think is more important? Why?
- Does the idea of a "sacred word" to express your love and longing for God make sense to you? Do you believe such a word could express your faith and trust in God and help you control distractions during contemplative prayer? Why or why not? Do you think using such a word as described in this book can lead you into a deep interior silence where God is known in love? Explain.

Journaling Suggestions

- If you have ever had a "crisis of faith," describe it in your journal. Has it been resolved? If so, how? If not, what resources are available to see you through your crisis of faith?
- Reflect on your life. How much time do you spend rehashing the past? Rehearsing the future? Living in the present moment? In what ways might the practice of contemplative prayer ground you more in the present moment?
- Now that you have come to the end of this book, write about what you have learned and experienced with respect to prayer. How has your practice changed? Where will you go next on the path of prayer?

Ideas for Practice

- Practice, practice, practice, but be sure to stay in conversation with a spiritual director or spiritual friend about your experience with contemplative prayer.
- Take your sacred word with you into the day. If you are walking to, waiting for, or riding on the bus, repeat the word in rhythm with your breathing. If you are doing anything that doesn't require thought, like washing the dishes, walking the dog, cutting the grass, waiting in the grocery line, silently repeat your word. It will bring a sense of equanimity and peacefulness, and will deepen both your sense of interior silence and your awareness of God's presence in the events and interactions of daily life.

FOR FURTHER READING

On Prayer

Anonymous. *The Cloud of Unknowing and Other Works*, trans. Clifton Wolters, London: Penguin Books, 1978.

Bondi, Roberta C. *To Pray and to Love: Conversations on Prayer with the Early Church*, Minneapolis: Fortress Press, 1991.

Finley, James. *Christian Meditation: Experiencing the Presence of God*, San Francisco: HarperSanFrancisco, 2004.

French, Henry F. *Book of Faith Lenten Journey: 40-Days with the Lord's Prayer*, Minneapolis: Augsburg Fortress Publishers, 2008.

Hallesby, Ole. *Prayer*, Minneapolis: Augsburg Fortress Publishers, 1994.

Keating, Thomas. *Open Heart, Open Mind: The Contemplative Dimension of the Gospel*, Warwick, N.Y.: Amity House, 1986.

Keating, Thomas M. Basil Pennington, Thomas E. Clarke. *Finding Grace at the Center: The Beginning of Centering Prayer*, Woodstock, Vt.: SkyLight Paths Publishing, 2002.

Koenig, John. *Rediscovering New Testament Prayer: Boldness and Blessing in the Name of Jesus*, Harrisburg, Penn.: Morehouse Publishing, 1998.

Main, John. *Essential Writings, Selected with an Introduction by Laurence Freeman*, Maryknoll, N.Y., Orbis Books, 2006.

Meadow, Mary Jo, Kevin Culligan, Daniel Chowning. *Christian Insight Meditation: Following in the Footsteps of John of the Cross*, Boston: Wisdom Publications, 2007.

Merton, Thomas. *Contemplative Prayer*, New York: Doubleday Image Books, 1971.

Merton, Thomas. *Spiritual Direction and Meditation and What Is Contemplation*, Wheathampstead, England: Anthony Clarke, 1975

Nesser, Joann. *Contemplative Prayer: Praying When the Well Runs Dry*, Minneapolis: Augsburg Books, 2007.

Pennington, M. Basil. *Centering Prayer: Renewing an Ancient Christian Prayer Form*, New York: Doubleday Image Books, 2001.

Yancy, Philip. *Prayer: Does It Make Any Difference?* Grand Rapids, Mich.: Zondervan, 2006.

On Jesus

Borg, Marcus. *Jesus: Uncovering the Life, Teachings, and Relevance of a Religious Revolutionary*, New York: HarperOne, 2008.

Borg, Marcus. *Meeting Jesus Again for the First Time: The Historical Jesus and the Heart of Contemporary Faith*, New York: HarperOne, 1995.

On the Bible

Borg, Marcus. *Reading the Bible Again For the First Time: Taking the Bible Seriously But Not Literally*, San Francisco: HarperSanFrancisco, 2001.

Various Authors. *Augsburg Commentary on the New Testament*, 15 volumes, Minneapolis: Augsburg Fortress Publishers.

Various Authors. *New Interpreters Bible Commentary*, 12 volumes, Nashville, Tenn.: Abingdon Press.

On Journaling

Hinchman, Hannah. *A Trail Through Leaves: The Journal as a Path to Place*, New York: W. W. Norton, 1997.

Klug, Ronald. *How to Keep a Spiritual Journal: A Guide to Journal Keeping for Inner Growth and Personal Discovery*, Minneapolis: Augsburg Books, 1993.

NOTES

1. Mary Schindler (1841), words in the public domain.

2. The Greek word translated in the NRSV as "among" is ambiguous. It can also be translated as "within." I suspect both meanings are appropriate.

3. Julian of Norwich, *Showings*, trans. and ed. Edmund Colledge, O.S.A. and James Walsh, S.J., Classics of Western Spirituality Series (Mahwah, N.J.: Paulist Press, 1978), 225.

4. Rainer Marie Rilke, *Letters to a Young Poet* (Mineola, N.Y.: Dover Publications, 2002), 35.

5. Shunryo Suzuki, *Zen Mind, Beginner's Mind* (Boston: Shambhala Publications, 2006), 2.

6. Henry French, *Book of Faith Lenten Journey: 40-Days with the Lord's Prayer* (Minneapolis: Augsburg Fortress, 2008), 20.

7. Martin Luther, "The Small Catechism," in *The Book of Concord*, eds. Robert Kolb and Timothy Wengert (Minneapolis: Fortress Press, 2000), 356. Emphasis added.

8. French, *Book of Faith Lenten Journal*, 70-71.

9. Ibid., 84.

10. Elizabeth Barrett Browning, *Aurora Leigh and Other Poems* (Whitefish, Mont.: Kessinger Publishing, 2004), 217.

11. Thomas Merton, *Thoughts in Solitude* (New York: Farrar, Straus, and Giroux, 1956), 83.

12. Julian of Norwich, *Showings*, 225.

13. John Donne, from Meditation 17, 1624.

14. Ronald Klug, *How To Keep A Spiritual Journal* (Minneapolis: Augsburg Books, 1993), 11.

15. Brother Lawrence, *The Practice of the Presence of God*, available on the Internet at http://www.practicegodspresence.com/brotherlawrence/practicegodspresence08.html. Accessed December 26, 2008.

16. See, for example:
http://www.worldprayers.org/frameit.cgi?/archive/prayers/celebrations/may_you_be_filled_with.html. Accessed December 26, 2008.

17. Michael Cooper-White, *The Comeback God* (Minneapolis: Augsburg Fortress, 2009), 41.

18. Thomas Merton, *Contemplative Prayer* (New York: Doubleday Image Books, 1971), 30.

19. *The American Heritage® Dictionary of the English Language, Third Edition* copyright © 1992 by Houghton Mifflin Company. Electronic version licensed from InfoSoft International, Inc. All rights reserved. (Emphasis added).

20. For an example of meditating on icons, see Henri J. M. Nouwen, *Behold the Beauty of the Lord: Praying with Icons* (Notre Dame, Ind.: Ave Maria Press, 1987).

21. Anonymous, *The Cloud of Unknowing and Other Works* (London: Penguin Books, 1978), 69.

22. Ibid.

23. John Main, *Essential Writings,* selected by Laurence Freeman (Maryknoll, N.Y.: Orbis Books, 2002), 98.

24. Merton, *Thoughts in Solitude*, 46.